JOSHUA

Living Word BIBLE STUDIES

JOSHUA

All God's Good Promises

KATHLEEN BUSWELL NIELSON

P&R PUBLISHING

P.O. BOX 817 • PHILLIPSBURG • NEW JERSEY 08865-0817

CONTENTS

CONTENTS

FOREWORD

Joshua is a challenging book to study, teach, and apply to daily Christian discipleship. I know this because my family has read it together for devotions after dinner—all seven of us, from age three to age forty-something.

There are some exciting battles in the book of Joshua. There are also some very long lists of people and places with strange-sounding names. What are we supposed to learn from this part of the Bible? What relationship does the book of Joshua have with the person and work of Jesus Christ? How does it help us in everyday life?

As a family we learned at least two important lessons from Joshua. The first is never to make any compromises with sin. Just as Joshua was called to fight a physical battle for every square inch of the Promised Land, we are called to fight a spiritual battle for every square inch of our souls. The second lesson is that there is a place for every one of God's children in the everlasting kingdom of God. Just as God gave a special piece of the Promised Land to every Israelite, he is preparing a special place for us in heaven.

You will learn these and many other valuable lessons as you read Joshua with the help of this study guide. The book of Joshua is a treasury of sacred truth. We know this because of everything the Bible says about itself. It is the very Word of God, breathed out by the Holy Spirit (2 Tim. 3:16-17). The one true and living God speaks to us in every word on every page. Thus we should believe that as we read and study the Bible we are hearing the voice of God.

This God-given Word was written by real human beings, who wrote under the direction of God the Holy Spirit (see 2 Peter 1:21). The Bible was written for people like us, by people like us. We should read the Bible, therefore, both as a divine book and as a human book. This means recognizing and understanding the conventional literary forms in which the Bible is written, finding pleasure and taking delight in the Bible's beauty, simplicity, and majesty. It also means that we should take as much care to study the Bible as the original authors took to write it, paying close attention to every word that was carefully chosen to fit into its proper context.

The Bible claims further that the Word of God is something we need to live, as much or even more than we need our daily bread (Matt. 4:4; cf. Deut. 8:3). Therefore, we should read and study the Bible every day as if our lives depended upon it.

To be more specific, the Bible has the life-giving power to bring us into a saving relationship with Jesus Christ (2 Tim. 3:15). The saving wisdom of Scripture is not limited to one part of the Bible or another, but holds true for every book in the Old and New Testaments, including the book of Joshua. As we read and study this part of the Bible, therefore, we see Jesus on every page. In Joshua we see him as the warrior of our salvation, the mighty captain of our faith, who will conquer all our enemies so that we can live in the Promised Land of his glory.

The Bible is also a practical book—a lamp to our feet and a light to our path (Ps. 119:105). The Bible tells us everything we need for godly thinking and holy living (2 Tim. 3:16-17). It shows us the way to go in life. In short, the Bible is the most useful book ever written. As we read, therefore, we should be looking for practical truth that will make a difference in what we think, what we say, and what we do in every situation in life.

This study guide will give you a helpful method for studying the Bible in all the right ways. It will encourage you in the daily reading, meditation, and memorization of Scripture. It will help you to be serious and systematic about studying the Bible for yourself. It will ask you questions that help you see the literary structure, the Christ-centered meaning, and the practical implications of the book of Joshua. It will give you growing skill and confidence in understanding the Bible, while at the same time helping you make progress in personal holiness and deepening your love for God the Father, God the Son, and God the Holy Spirit. And it will help you do all of this in relationship with other members of your spiritual family—your brothers and sisters in the church.

May the same Holy Spirit who first revealed these words enable you to understand what you read, find joy in what you study, trust more deeply in Jesus Christ, and return the glory to God by the way that you live.

Philip Graham Ryken

A Personal Word
from Kathleen

I began to write these Bible studies for the women in my own church group at College Church in Wheaton, Illinois. Under the leadership of Kent and Barbara Hughes, the church and that Bible study aimed to proclaim without fail the good news of the Word of God. What a joy, in that study and in many since, to see lives changed by the work of the Word, by the Spirit, for the glory of Christ.

In our Bible study group, we were looking for curriculum that would lead us into the meat of the Word and teach us how to take it in, whole Bible books at a time—the way they are given to us in Scripture. Finally, one of our leaders said, "Kathleen—how about if you just write it!" And so began one of the most joyful projects of my life: the writing of studies intended to help unleash the Word of God in people's lives. The writing began during a busy stage of my life—with three lively young boys and always a couple of college English courses to teach—but through that stage and every busy one since, a serious attention to studying the Bible has helped keep me focused, growing, and alive in the deepest ways. The Word of God will do that. If there's life and power in these studies, it is simply the life and power of the Scriptures to which they point. It is ultimately the life and power of the Savior who shines through all the Scriptures from beginning to end. How we need this life, in the midst of every busy and non-busy stage of our lives!

I don't think it is just the English teacher in me that leads me to this conclusion about our basic problem in Bible study these days: we've forgotten how to *read*! We're so used to fast food that we think we should be able to drive by the Scriptures periodically and pick up some easily digestible truths that someone else has wrapped up neatly for us. We've disowned that process of careful reading . . . observing the words . . . seeing the shape of a book and a passage . . . asking questions that take us into the text rather than away from it . . . digging into the Word and letting it speak! Through such a process, guided by the Spirit, the Word of God truly feeds our souls. Here's my prayer: that, by means of these studies, people would be further enabled to read the Scriptures profitably and thereby find life and nourishment in them, as we are each meant to do.

In all the busy stages of life and writing, I have been continually surrounded by pastors, teachers, and family who encourage and help me in this work, and for that I am grateful. The most wonderful guidance and encouragement come from my husband, Niel, whom I thank and for whom I thank God daily.

May God use these studies to lift up Christ and his Word, for his glory!

Introduction

The book of Joshua offers adventure, great stories, vivid characters, and—above all—an amazing account of the way God fulfills his promises to his people. Joshua is not bare history; it is history with a point—and the point is that God's Word is true—always, completely, without fail. This book's challenge is for God's people to live according to that Word.

Joshua opens the second section of the Scriptures, which in the Hebrew Bible is called the Former Prophets. However, Joshua also gives a kind of epilogue to the Bible's first section, the Pentateuch (the five books of Moses). The story fulfilled in Joshua begins in Genesis, as God created a race of people to live with him and glorify him. As Genesis tells it, the first human beings God created rebelled against him and caused the race to be a fallen one, separated from its holy Creator. But God, even as he judged this rebellion, gave a promise—a promise that Satan, who lured Adam and Eve into rebellion, would ultimately be conquered by the seed of a woman (Gen. 3:15). God chose one man through whom to channel this promise: Abraham, he said, would be the one through whom this seed would come. Out of Abraham would come a great nation through whom the whole earth would be blessed, and God promised to give that nation the land of Canaan for their own (Gen. 12:1–7). Abraham went and lived in that land, but after several generations his extended family moved to Egypt, where his descendant Joseph had risen to great political power. Abraham's people flourished there and grew numerous, just as God had said. In fact, they grew so numerous that they were feared and made a nation of slaves. Not until Moses' time were they delivered and brought back as a whole nation of God's people through the wilderness to their own land. Moses brought them to the brink of the land, but he was not allowed to take them in; Joshua was appointed as the leader for the conquest of the land of Canaan. Moses brought them out, and Joshua will bring them in. *The book of Joshua is the story of God's bringing his redeemed people into the land he promised them.*

Joshua, then, gives the happy end to the story of God's people. But, as the Bible goes on, we soon see that this was only a hint of the *very* end of the story. Even in Joshua itself there are clear warning signs that all is not completely well. But in Judges, the next book, those warnings prove all too true. After all God has provided for them, his people will not obey him and settle happily in the land he has provided. It is clear that the promised seed of Abraham who will finally accomplish the happy ending has not yet come. The deliverance from slavery in Egypt on that night of the Passover turns out to be a wonderful hint of the deliverance still to come—and it will come only through Jesus Christ, the true seed, the real Passover Lamb. The wilderness wanderings turn out to be an all-too-recognizable hint of the life journeys of God's people, graciously given his law but struggling to obey it. Only the true seed, Jesus Christ, was able to face temptation in the wilderness and never sin—for he relied on the true manna from heaven (Matt. 4:2–4). And the final inheritance of Canaan turns out to be a beautiful hint of the eternal inheritance and rest God gives to his people—both now, as we know rest for our souls through Christ the Lord and Savior, and eternally, in heaven. Canaan ultimately points toward the final, joyful rest in the presence of Jesus Christ, the certain hope and promised inheritance of everyone who trusts in him. The name Joshua means "the Lord saves," and in its Greek form is translated Jesus. Joshua was a great leader who faithfully and obediently delivered his people. But both Joshua and the book named after him point clearly ahead to Jesus Christ, the one who would finally and perfectly save his people, giving them an inheritance that will never perish, spoil, or fade (1 Peter 1:3–5).

Joshua, then, stands at a pivotal point in Scripture, looking back to and confirming God's word in the Pentateuch, but also looking far forward to the final fulfillment of all God's good promises. Who wrote this masterful book? Scripture does not directly name the author of Joshua. The tradition of centuries holds that Joshua himself wrote most of it. Certainly passages like Joshua 24:25–26 show Joshua writing down records in the Book of the Law of God. Joshua's authorship is confirmed by the fact that much of the story is told with vivid, seemingly firsthand detail and immediacy. It is generally agreed that careful editors finished and perhaps gave final, unifying touches to the book in ensuing years. In any case, what we can and must affirm is that this book offers a true, inspired account of the fulfillment of God's promises to his people. God is the final author of this book, and he is the main character as well, for in Joshua it is God who acts to deliver and to settle his people according to his powerful word. "Not one word of all the good promises that the LORD had made to the house of Israel had failed; all came to pass," Joshua 21:45 tells us. This book is the account of a powerful, faithful, covenant-keeping God.

We can understand this book adequately just by following the narrative in Joshua itself. But we will understand it a great deal better with a bit of helpful context. The lessons in this study do refer to other books in the Bible, especially the five books that precede Joshua. Deuteronomy, for example, contains Moses' final presentation of God's law to the people; it is that law which Joshua aims to follow and live out, every step of the way. It will be helpful, if Bible study is new to you, to find the table of contents in the Bible you are using and to be ready to use it to locate other biblical books. New Testament books will be referenced as well, as we look to find the final fulfillment of all God's good promises in the Lord Jesus Christ. Maps, too, are provided in order to make more vivid these stories of entering the land. At certain points, the lessons recommend looking at particular maps; throughout the study, however, you will benefit from regularly checking the maps to find the places mentioned in the stories.

The point of such a study as this is to allow the Word of God to speak to us today. God's promises are just as good and true for God's people now as they were in Joshua's day. His Word has been completed and fulfilled in Jesus Christ, and we have the privilege of holding the whole Bible in our hands and personally knowing the Lord to whom it all points. May we know the Lord Jesus Christ better through this study; may we learn more of what it means to trust and obey God's Word; may we find hope in all his good promises.

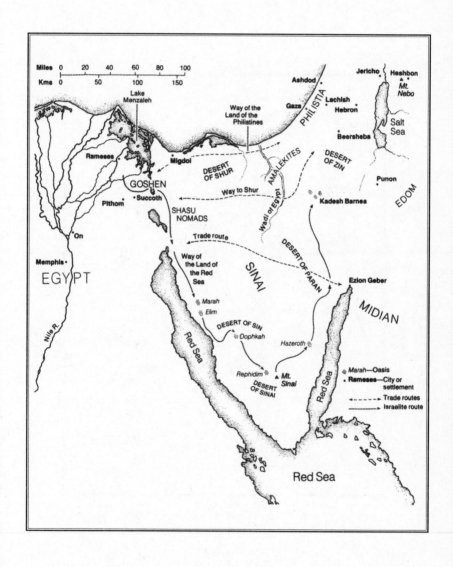

MAP 1: ROUTE OF THE EXODUS

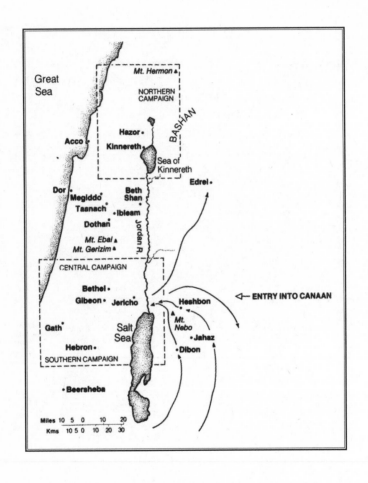

MAP 2: CONQUEST OF CANAAN

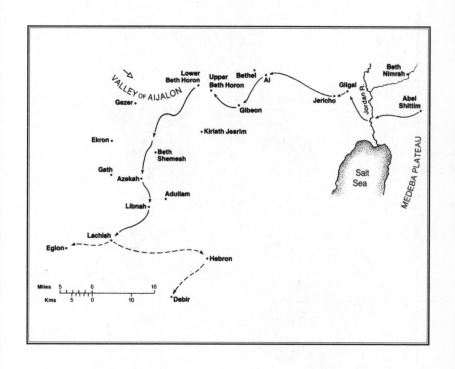

MAP 3: THE CENTRAL CAMPAIGN

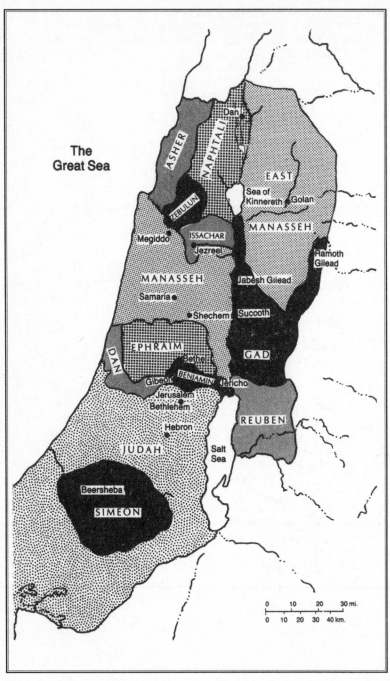

The
Great Sea

ASHER

NAPHTALI

Dan

EAST

Sea of
Kinnereth   Golan

ZEBULUN

MANASSEH

Megiddo

ISSACHAR

Jezreel

Ramoth
Gilead

MANASSEH

Jabesh Gilead

Samaria

Shechem   Succoth

EPHRAIM

DAN

Bethel

GAD

Gibeon   BENJAMIN   Jericho

Jerusalem
Bethlehem

Hebron

REUBEN

Salt
Sea

JUDAH

Beersheba

SIMEON

0   10   20   30 mi.

0   10   20   30   40 km.

MAP 4: LAND OF THE TWELVE TRIBES

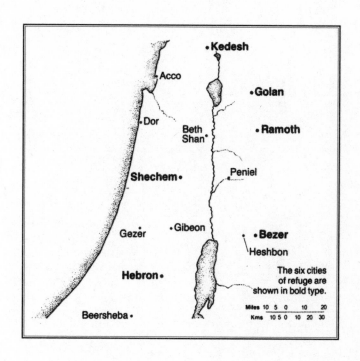

The six cities
of refuge are
shown in bold type.

MAP 5: CITIES OF REFUGE

Lesson 1 (Josh. 1)
GOD GIVES THE WORD

Opening the book of Joshua, we first hear God speaking to this newly commissioned leader of Israel. God's word is what he has given and what he continues to give his people as they stand on the brink of the promised land. We will do well to listen carefully as God speaks and as Joshua and the people respond; like them, may we grasp the power and the primary importance of God's Word. Because this book continues a much larger story, in this first lesson especially we will spend some time looking back to clarify the context in which Joshua comes to us.

DAY ONE—THE CONTINUING WORD
(JOSH. 1:1–5)

1. The opening verses remind us that this book continues a huge story in progress. Write down any phrases from Joshua 1:1–5 that refer to past events.

   AFTER THE DEATH

   AS I PROMISED

   AS I WAS WITH MOSES

2. That first phrase, "after the death of Moses," connects us directly to the end of the previous book. Turn back a few pages and read Deuteronomy 34. What other connections with Joshua 1:1–5 do you find in Deuteronomy 34?

VS 4 THE LAND I PROMISED
5 MOSES THE SERVANT
5 MOSES DIED THERE AS THE LORD SAID
9 JOSHUA FILLED WITH THE SPIRIT
   OF WISDOM
9 ISRAELITES LISTENED TO JOSHUA
10-12 THE LORD SENT MOSES + HE DID
   AWESOME THINGS

3. Deuteronomy 34:4 connects us to God's previous, repeated promise of the land. Trace this promise through the following representative verses, jotting down brief observations concerning God's promise to establish his people in the land of Canaan.

   a. Genesis 12:1–7 Go...
      GOD WILL MAKE ABRAM INTO A GREAT NATION
      HE BLESS THEM + MAKE THEIR NAME GREAT
      + THEY WILL BE A BLESSING!
      ALL PEOPLES WILL BE BLESSED THROUGH
      ABRAM.
      7 - GOD SAID: TO YOUR OFFSPRING I WILL GIVE
      THIS LAND

   b. Genesis 15:1–16
V-1 GOD SAID: DO NOT BE AFRAID, I AM YOUR
   SHIELD, YOUR VERY GREAT REWARD.
V6 - BELIEF → RIGHTEOUSNESS
12-16 REVELATION OF FUTURE FULFILLMENT
   OF PROMISE.

2

c. Genesis 26:2-3

SPECIFIC INSTRUCTION FROM GOD

V 3-STAY... I'M WITH YOU... I WILL BLESS YOU

  4 - DESCENDENTS = STARS, HE WILL GIVE THEM THE LAND, + ALL NATIONS WILL BE BLESSED.

d. Genesis 28:10-13

V 12-JACOB'S DREAM

  LORD REVEALS HIMSELF IN DREAM

V 13 SAYS HE WILL GIVE JACOB + HIS DESCENDENTS THE LAND ON WHICH HE IS LAYING.

e. Exodus 3:7-8

  LORD SEE'S THE MISERY OF HIS PEOPLE

V 7 - IN EGYPT; HE HEARS THEIR CRYING + IS CONCERNED ABOUT THEIR SUFFERING,

  8- HE HAS COME DOWN TO RESCUE THEM OUT OF THAT LAND INTO A GOOD + SPACIOUS LAND

f. Numbers 26:52-56

THE LAND IS ALLOTTED TO ISRAEL AS AN INHERITANCE

g. Deuteronomy 1:6-8

GO (TIMES UP)
INTO THE HILL COUNTRY
LORD HAS GIVEN LAND TO THEM.
GO + TAKE POSESSION OF LAND
    HE PROMISED TO THEIR FATHERS.

h. Joshua 1:3-4

THE LORD GAVE THEM THE LAND
    EVERY WHERE THEY SET FOOT
FROM THE DESERT TO LEBANON
FROM EUPHRATES TO THE MEDITER-
RANEAN.
[A MEASURE OF VASTNESS YET SPEC-
    IFIC; DEFINED BOUNDARY]

4. In what ways does this historical perspective expand
   your understanding of God?

GOD HAS PLANS FOR HIS PEOPLE.
GOD PROMISES SPECIFIC GOOD
GOD'S PLANS AND PROMISES ARE
    NOT THWARTED.
GOD KEEPS HIS PROMISES.
GOD IS PATIENT, FAITHFUL,
    AT WORK EVEN WHEN WE
    ARE UNAWARE.
GOD'S PLANS + PROMISES ARE
    GOOD FOR HIS PEOPLE BUT
    NOT JUST HIS PEOPLE. HIS
    PURPOSE OF BLESSING HIS PEOPLE
    IS THAT THEY WILL BE A BLESSING
    TO OTHERS (ALL NATIONS)

QUESTION:

DAY TWO—FOLLOWING JOSHUA
THROUGH THE WORD

1. "Joshua the son of Nun" (Josh. 1:1) carried with him much personal experience of this history. He had been "assistant" (v. 1) to Moses, the one who wrote it all down in the Pentateuch (the Bible's first five books, called the Books of Moses or the Law). According to the following passages from the Pentateuch, in what ways had God prepared Joshua for this call to action in Joshua 1?

   a. Exodus 17:8–16

   MOSES GAVE JOSHUA RESPONSIBILITY + LEADERSHIP, TRUST + TRAINING; AUTHORITY + DECISION MAKING.

   b. Exodus 24:12–18

   MOSES HAD JOSHUA ACCOMPANY HIM UP ON MT SINAI. HE GAVE JOSHUA THE TABLETS OF STONE WITH THE LAW + COMMANDMENTS WRITTEN ON THEM. MOSES TRUSTED JOSHUA.

   c. Exodus 33:7–11

   JOSHUA REMAINED AT THE TENT OF MEETING, EVEN WHEN MOSES LEFT.

d. Numbers 11:24–30

MOSES TAUGHT / MENTORED /
CORRECTED JOSHUA.

e. Numbers 13:16

MOSES NAMED 'JOSHUA'

f. Numbers 14:6–9, 26–35

JOSHUA (+ CALEB) SAW THE GOOD LAND.
THEY BELIEVED GOD WOULD GIVE IT
TO THEM IF ~~THE~~ HE WAS PLEASED
WITH THEM. AND BECAUSE OF THIS
THEY WERE NOT AFRAID. MOSES
RECOGNIZED THE FAITH + COURAGE IN
JOSHUA. MOSES TRUSTED JOSHUA'S REPORT

g. Numbers 27:12–23

MOSES OBEYED GOD AND COMMISSIONED
JOSHUA WITH AUTHORITY TO LEAD
GOD'S PEOPLE T° GO OUT + TO COME IN.

2. In one sentence, summarize what Joshua had been privileged to learn about God through all these experiences.

JOSHUA LEARNED GOD IS HOLY + PRESENT
AND THAT HE PREPARED JOSHUA TO
HELP FULFILL HIS PROMISES TO HIS
PEOPLE.

3. Because it's all been written down in Scripture, we, too, are privileged to learn and believe these things about God. How might reading of Joshua's preparation experiences help prepare you for what you face today or in days to come?

BELIEVING GOD IS HOLY, PRESENT
AND WORKING HIS PLAN. HE HAS
PREPARED ME TO JOIN HIM IN HIS
MISSION, UTILIZING THE GIFTS +
STRENGTHS GOD HAS GIVEN ME.

DAY THREE—GOD SPEAKS COMMANDS AND ENCOURAGEMENTS (JOSH. 1:1–9)

God had clearly been at work through centuries of preparation for this "Now therefore" of Joshua 1:2. So—now therefore, finally, it's time to "arise" and "go" (v. 2).

1. List all the commands given by God to Joshua in 1:1–9.

GET READY TO CROSS JORDAN RIVER
BE STRONG + COURAGEOUS
LEAD THE PEOPLE INTO THE PROMISED LAND
BE STRONG + VERY COURAGEOUS
OBEY THE LAW; DO NOT TURN FROM IT R/L
KEEP THE LAW ON YOUR LIPES
MEDITATE ON THE LAW DAY + NIGHT
DO NOT BE DISCOURAGED

2a. The "law" given by Moses (v. 7) and the "Book of the Law" (v. 8) refer to the Pentateuch, the inspired word written by Moses. What do you notice about the commands specifically relating to the written word of God (Josh. 1:7–8)?

TO OBEY THE LAW + NOT TURN
FROM IT TO THE LEFT OR RIGHT.
KNOW + SPEAK THE LAW.
MEDITATE ON THE LAW DAY + NIGHT

b. How do these commands apply to us?

THE COMMANDS INSTRUCT ME
ON WHAT TO DO AND INDICATE
THE VALUE GOD HAS OF THE LAW.

3. Each time God commands Joshua to "be strong and courageous," he links the command to a different encouragement. What kinds of encouragements do you find in the following verses?

a. Joshua 1:6

• BECAUSE OF GOD'S PLAN + PURPOSE

•

b. Joshua 1:7

- THE OBEDIENCE+STEADFASTNESS TO THE LAW IS FOUNDATIONAL TO BEING STRONG + ~~&~~ COURAGEOUS!

c. Joshua 1:9 (and v. 5)

DO NOT BE AFRAID OR DISCOURAGED BECAUSE GOD IS WITH JOSHUA.

4. How marvelous to see a God who clearly commands and personally encourages his people. What specifically encourages you in these verses so far? How or why?

GOD'S PRESENCE; HIS PLANS AND PURPOSES. HE WILL NEVER LEAVE. HE GIVES HIS PEOPLE HIS SPIRIT + HIS WORD. HE EQUIPS HIS SERVANTS WITH WHAT THEY NEED TO OBEY.

Day Four—Joshua and the People
Respond (Josh. 1:10–15)

1. What do you notice about Joshua's response in Joshua 1:10–11?

   JOSHUA TOLD THE PEOPLE WHAT
   TO DO AND WHY. THEY ARE TO
   TAKE POSESSION OF GOD'S LONG
   PROMISED GIFT: THE LAND.

2. For background, read Numbers 32:1–33, in which two and a half tribes receive already-conquered territory east of the Jordan River. Now, in Joshua 1:12–15, which phrases show the authority by which Joshua is now speaking to these two and a half tribes?

   JOSHUA BEGAN + ENDED WITH
   REMINDER OF WHAT MOSES
   THE SERVANT OF THE LORD
   HAS SAID.

3. Whether Joshua 1:16–18 gives the response of the two and a half tribes or all the tribes, these words represent the right and good response of God's people to his word. How would you characterize their response?

   THEY RESPONDED WITH COMPLETE
   OBEDIENCE -TO DO AS COMMANDED,
   TO GO AS SENT. AND WORDS/ OF PRAYER
   BLESSING + PROTECTION FOR JOSHUA

4. What, specifically, challenges you as you see Joshua and then the people responding to the word given them from the Lord?

GOD COMMANDED ALL HIS PEOPLE THROUGH ONE PERSON. HE DEMANDED COMPLETE, COLLECTIVE OBEDIENCE. THAT IS HARD TO IMAGINE TODAY!

DAY FIVE—WE RESPOND, ACCORDING TO THE WORD

1. Look back to Joshua 1:13, 15 and back further to Exodus 33:14. What word appears in each of these three verses to describe what God gives his people in the land?

REST

2. Do people yearn for rest today? What kind of rest? How do they seek it?

YES, EVEN TODAY PEOPLE YEARN FOR REST. WE SEEK IT WITH "VACATIONS, SPA DAYS, ME TIME." WHAT KIND OF REST—PERHAPS PHYSICAL BUT OFTEN I THINK IT IS FROM THE BARAGE OF BURDENS.

3. In Scripture, rest is both the blessing and the end of the journey that begins with redemption and follows the direction of God's law (see the introduction). According to the following verses, what can you say about the rest God offers to those who believe his word and put their faith in him?

   a. Psalm 62:5–8

   REST IN GOD –
   • MY HOPE
   • MY ROCK
   • MY SALVATION
   • MY FORTRESS
   • MY REFUGE

   • I WON'T BE SHAKEN
   • HONOR DEPENDS ON HIM
   • TRUST IN HIM AT ALL TIMES
   • POUR MY HEART OUT TO HIM

   b. Matthew 11:28–29

   COME TO HIM ALL WHO ARE WEARY + BURDENED; TAKE HIS YOKE; LEARN FROM HIM; HE IS GENTLE + HUMBLE IN HEART. HIS YOKE IS EASY. HIS BURDEN IS LIGHT.

   c. Hebrews 3:16–4:11 (This is a beautiful but difficult passage; aim simply to get a central idea.)

   BELIEVERS ENTER HIS REST
   MAKE EVERY EFFORT TO ENTER THAT REST.

d. Revelation 21:1–5

NEW HEAVEN + EARTH WHERE
GOD DWELLS AMONG THE PEOPLE.
HE WIPES AWAY EVERY TEAR.
HE IS MAKING EVERYTHING NEW!

4. In believing and obeying the Word of the Lord, we
   find true rest, now and eternally, through our Lord and
   Redeemer Jesus Christ. Review again the life-and-death
   seriousness and the beautiful abandon of the people's
   response to the word of the Lord brought to them by
   Joshua (Josh. 1:16–18). Spend a few minutes in prayer,
   telling God your response to his Word.

Notes for Lesson 1

Lesson 2 (Josh. 2)

GOD SHOWS HIS MERCIFUL PLAN

As God's people prepare to enter and take the land, Joshua 2's glimpse into Jericho reminds us of God's merciful, far-reaching purposes at work. The story in Joshua reaches all the way to us.

DAY ONE—SPY OUT THE CHAPTER

For this first day, read through Joshua 2.

1. Begin by simply relishing the story.

2. Examine the chapter to see what shape or organization you find.

3. Finally, record any observations or questions that strike you on this first reading.

SPIES HIDE W/ A PROSTITUTE.

RAHAB SERVES AS INFORMANT + PROTECTOR WHO CARES DEEPLY FOR HER FAMILY.

RAHAB BELIEVES GOD'S FAVOR ON ISRAELITES.

SHE NEGOTIATES WITH SPIES.

SHE HIDES SPIES + LIES TO KING TO MISLEAD HIS MEN AS THEY SEARCH FOR SPIES.

SPIES RETURN TO JOSHUA + GIVE HIM REPORT ON PEOPLE OF JERICHO, BASED ON RAHAB'S INFORMATION.

Day Two—Contexts

1. Consider the story of Rahab and the spies in its immediate context, following directly after the narrative of Joshua 1. How is this narrative order important to the story and effective for the reader?

   BELIEVE GOD + OBEY HIM.
   JOSHUA BELIEVES, OBEYS + LEADS.
   GOD IS AT WORK BEHIND THE
      SCENES.
   THE SERVANT-SPIES ALSO SEEM
      TO BELIEVE + OBEY.

2. Read Joshua 2:1 and consider the geographical context of this part of the story. Consult maps #1, #2, and #3 to locate

   a. the Jordan River—the boundary to be crossed into the promised land (Josh. 1:2).

   b. Shittim (or Abel-shittim)—east of the Jordan River, where Israel was camped.

   c. Jericho—west of the Jordan River, a well-fortified city supplied by natural springs, strategic in controlling trade along the Jordan Valley and access into the hill country of Canaan.

3. Consider the context of the Pentateuch: spies had been sent forty years earlier, up from the south, with very different results. Look through Numbers 13:1–14:38; note several comparisons and contrasts you find between the former expedition and the present one.

   1) SPIES BELIEVED THE PEOPLE IN THE PROMISED LAND WERE TO POWERFUL TO ATTACK.

   2) FAITH IN THE LORD EVIDENT IN LIVES OF JOSHUA + CALEB, 2 OF 12 SPIES.

   3) ISRAELITES TALKED OF STONING J+C.

   4) THE ASSEMBLY DOUBTFUL OF GOD IN FIRST ACCOUNT; THEY BELIEVED GOD IN SECOND ACCOUNT.

   5) THE 10 WHO GAVE BAD REPORT DIED-STRUCK DOWN FOR NOT BELIEVING THE LORD.

4. Finally, consider the context of God's promises in relation to this story. How does each of the following find fulfillment in Joshua 2?

   a. Genesis 12:3

   RAHAB KNEW OF GOD'S FAVOR UPON THE ISRAELITES, AS WELL AS THE KING + ALL THE PEOPLE. ISRAEL'S NAME WAS GREAT!

   RAHAB BLESSED THE 2 SPIES SENT BY JOSHUA. IN TURN SHE + HER FAMILY WERE BLESSED.

b.   Exodus 15:13–16

GOD LEAD HIS PEOPLE, THOSE HE
REDEEMED. HIS PRESENCE IN HIS
PEOPLE CAUSED THE NATIONS TO
TREMBLE, ALLOWING HIS PEOPLE TO
PASS BY.

Day Three—Rahab . . . The Heart of the Story (Josh. 2:8–13)

1. In the midst of all these contexts emerges the central
   figure of Rahab the prostitute. First, carefully study her
   beautiful, central speech to the spies (Josh. 2:9–13).
   Using specific verses for support, make a list of what
   Rahab knows about God.

V-9   1) HE HAS GIVEN THEM THE LAND

V-10 2) THE LORD DRIED UP THE WATER
         IN THE RED SEA

V-11 3) ISRAEL'S GOD IS GOD IN HEAVEN
         ABOVE + ON EARTH BELOW.

2. What is the difference between the response of Rahab and that of the people around her?

THE PEOPLE AROUND RAHAB ARE MELTING IN FEAR, THEIR COURAGE FAILED.

RAHAB PROFESSED HER BELIEF OF WHO GOD IS, EMPHASIZING HIS POWER AND PROTECTION OF HIS PEOPLE. SHE WAS NOT AFRAID RATHER SOUGHT PROTECTION FROM THE GOD OF HEAVEN + EARTH.

3. Rahab, an unbelieving prostitute in an unbelieving land, was given a heart of faith in the one true God. What do the New Testament writers celebrate about her faith?

~870 YEARS LATER!

a. Hebrews 11:31

SHE WELCOMED THE SPIES. SHE WAS OBEDIENT, NOT DISOBEDIENT.

b. James 2:20–26

HER FAITH WAS ACCOMPANIED BY HER DEEDS.

4. Find Rahab in Matthew 1:1–17. What is so wonderful about finding her there?

RAHAB WAS THE WIFE OF ~~SOLUTION~~ SALMON AND THE MOTHER OF BOAZ! SHE IS PART OF THE GENEOLOGY OF JESUS HERE ON EARTH!

5. Summarize what this story of Rahab is teaching us about God and what he is like.

FAITH, THE ACTIVE + RESPONSIVE KIND, IS MORE IMPORTANT OR AS IMPORTANT THAN HERITAGE + BLOODLINE. GOD IS GREATER THAN OUR SIN. A HEART THAT RESPONDS TO HIM IN FAITH TRANSCENDS OUR PRESUPPOSITIONS, UNDERSTANDING, AND TRADITION. GOD WILL NOT BE BOUND BY SUCH HUMAN CONFINES. WE DO NOT LIKE THE WIND, KNOW WHERE THE SPIRIT OF THE LORD WILL GO!

DAY FOUR—RAHAB IN ACTION
(JOSH. 2:2–7, 15–16, 22, 1, 23–24)

1. We have seen that the New Testament celebrates Rahab's faith in action (day 3, question 3). How does Joshua 2:2–3 highlight this courageous action?

RAHAB'S HOSPITALITY CAUGHT THE
ATTENTION OF THE KING! HE GAVE
SPECIFIC COMMANDS FOR HE TO
FOLLOW RE THE SPIES.

2. Rahab's response to the king's messengers has been much debated. God's law commands his people not to give false testimony against their neighbors (Ex. 20:16). What do you make of Rahab's lie, as it is given to us in this story (Josh. 2:4–7)?

WAS SHE BOUND AT THAT POINT
BY GOD'S LAW? SHE ALSO WAS A
PROSTITUTE. COULD IT BE THAT
SHE KNEW THAT A GOD WHO
HAD NOT BEEN HER GOD WAS
REVEALING HIMSELF TO BE THE
GOD (OF HEAVEN + EARTH)?

3. Scripture commends Rahab for welcoming and protecting the spies. How does Joshua 2:15–16, 22 let us grasp the picture more completely?

SHE KNEW THE NORMS OF HER PEOPLE, THE CULTURE. SHE WAS INSTRUMENT OF PROTECTION FOR THE MEN THE LORD SENT INTO THE PROMISED LAND.

4. Review the book-end verses of the story (Josh. 2:1, 23–24). What was the most important gift with which Rahab allowed the spies to return to Joshua?

RENEWED FAITH THAT GOD WAS GIVING THE LAND INTO THEIR HANDS. ONE OF THOSE "THIS MUST BE GOD" MOMENTS, A DIVINE APPOINTMENT WITH RAHAB, POSSIBLY THE ONLY 'MAN OF PEACE' IN ALL OF JERICHO.

Day Five—The Far-Reaching Cord of Mercy
(Josh. 2:12–14, 17–21)

1. Read Joshua 2:12–14. *Hesed,* the Hebrew word used twice in 2:12 and once in 2:14, is variously translated "kindness," "steadfast love," "unfailing love," or "mercy." *Hesed* abounds in the Old Testament in reference to God's merciful love for his people. Look at Exodus 12:1–13, and then read Joshua 6:22–25. In what ways is the *hesed* of God similar in these two stories?

   FAITH. OBEDIENCE - PASSOVER
   WOW! GOD SPARED RAHAB FROM
   DESTRUCTION BECAUSE OF HER
   FAITH + ACTION RE THE SPIES.

2. In Rahab's story, we see God extending his mercy to the nations, even as he promised. That promise reaches all the way to us. As you prayerfully read the following verses, write down ways in which God's steadfast love and mercy extend to you.

   a. Ephesians 2:1–10

   HESED - I BROUGHT NOTHING TO THE
   TABLE OF GOD'S SALVATION EXCEPT
   MY SIN + SEPARATION FROM HIM.
   HE BROUGHT EVERYTHING! LOVE, MERCY,
   LIFE IN CHRIST, GRACE, RAISED IN CHRIST,
   SEATED WITH HIM IN THE HEAVENLY
   REALMS, AS A CONTINUED DEMONSTRATION
   OF HIS GRACE, KINDNESS, NOT BY
   WORK BUT BY FAITH!

b. Titus 3:3–7

HESED-IN MY SIN + DISOBEDIENCE
HE CAME TO ME WITH MERCY,
GRACE, JUSTIFICATION IN CHRIST,
RENEWED BY THE HOLY SPIRIT, MADE
ME AN HEIR, ETERNAL LIFE!

c. 1 Peter 2:9–10

CHOSEN, ROYAL PRIESTHOOD, GOD'S
SPECIAL POSSESION, OF GOD'S PEOPLE
AND SHOWN MERCY!

Notes for Lesson 2

Lesson 3 (Josh. 3-4)

GOD BROUGHT THEM OUT— KEEP TELLING IT!

While Rahab waits with the scarlet cord hanging in her window, the narrative moves back to the Israelites and, in Joshua 3-4, shows them crossing the Jordan River. May this story, as it is retold among us, once again inspire a wondrous fear of the Lord, whose powerful hand ushers his people into the land.

DAY ONE—THE STORY DOES NOT GO STRAIGHT ACROSS!

Read through the amazing story of the crossing in Joshua 3-4. Clearly, the Hebrew narrative method does not emphasize a logical or chronological order. What parts of the story does Joshua seem to emphasize as he circles through the events of the crossing? Write down your observations and questions.

THE PRESENCE OF GOD
THE POWER OF GOD
THE PROTECTION OF GOD

THE AFFIRMATION OF JOSHUA
   AS LEADER OF ISRAELITES

THE EXULTATION OF JOSHUA
CHOSEN BY GOD — GOD IS WITH JOSHUA
                PEOPLE WILL KNOW

THE FAITH + OBEDIENCE OF
   JOSHUA TO THE LORD

Day Two—The Ark at the Story's Center

1. From God's instructions to Moses in Exodus 25:10–22, what do we know about what the ark of the covenant was and what it signified? *Note: The stone tablets inscribed with the Ten Commandments were the Testimony inside the ark.*

IT WAS AN OPULENT PORTABLE, PROTECTIVE DISPLAY CABINET FOR THE TESTIMONY OF GOD. PRECISE INSTRUCTIONS WERE GIVEN BY GOD TO MOSES FOR THE CONSTRUCTION OF THE ARK. ACACIA WOOD OVERLAYED INSIDE + OUT WITH GOLD, CONSTRUCTED FOR FUNCTION + ORNATE WITH MEANING.

2. Now, work through Joshua 3–4, listing all the observations you can make concerning the role of the ark in this story. Cite verse references with your observations.

CH 3

V 3 - CARRIED BY LEVITICAL PRIESTS; FOLLOW IT

V 4 - KNOW WHERE TO GO; KEEP A DISTANCE

V 6 - ARK TO BE CARRIED AHEAD OF PEOPLE

V 8 - ARK TO BE CARRIED INTO RIVER'S EDGE

V 11 - ARK WILL GO AHEAD OF YOU INTO JORDAN RIVER

V 13 - WHEN PRIESTS W/ ARK STEP INTO RIVER THE WATER WILL BE CUT OFF + STAND UP IN A HEAP

V 16 - WHILE ARK CARRIED INTO RIVER WATER STOPPED A GREAT DISTANCE AWAY

V 17 - PRIESTS STOOD ON DRY GROUND

CH 4

V 2 - GET LG STONES (12) IN FRONT OF ARK IN MIDDLE OF JORDAN RIVER.
WHEN ARK CARRIED OUT OF JORDAN RIVER WATERS RETURNED TO THEIR PLACE

3. Think carefully through these observations. What appear to be God's purposes in so focusing his people on the ark of the covenant as they cross the Jordan into the promised land?

- THAT THE LORD GOES BEFORE THEM (TO PLACES THEY HAVE NEVER BEEN BEFORE)
- THE HAND OF THE LORD IS POWERFUL
- TO ALWAYS FEAR THE LORD THEIR GOD
- THAT GOD IS WITH JOSHUA AS HE WAS WITH MOSES

4. In spite of popular movie lore, the ark is no longer with us and used by God in the same way. How does what the ark symbolized, however, remain crucial for us as God's people?

AS THE ARK WAS SO THE HOLY SPIRIT IS TODAY.

DAY THREE—THE PREPARATION
AND THE MIRACLE (JOSH. 3)

1. The people have been told they will cross the Jordan (Josh. 1:10–11). But they have not been told exactly how. God makes them go through certain stages of preparation in the several days preceding the crossing. According to the following verses, what kinds of preparations do you note, and what value would they have held for the people involved?

   a. Joshua 3:1–2a

   THEY APPROACHED THE JORDAN + THEN WAITED (CAMPED) FOR 3 DAYS.

   b. Joshua 3:3–4 WHEN THEY SEE ARK THEY'RE TO MOVE FROM POSITIONS AND FOLLOW IT.

c. Joshua 3:5 (see also Ex. 19:10–11; Num. 11:18)

THEY ARE TO CONSECRATE
THEMSELVES.

d. Joshua 3:7–8

THE LORD WILL EXALT JOSHUA IN THE
EYES OF ISRAL. HE WAS WITH JOSHUA
AS HE WAS WITH MOSES. GOD TOLD
JOSHUA THE INSTRUCTIONS TO BE
GIVEN TO THE PRIESTS.

e. Joshua 3:9–13

LISTEN. THE ARK WILL GO
AHEAD + THAT'S HOW YOU'LL
KNOW GOD IS WITH YOU

2. What details in Joshua 3:14–17 make God's miracle even more to be wondered at?

THE RIVER WAS AT FLOOD STAGE. AS SOON AS THE FEET OF THE PRIESTS TOUCHED THE WATER'S EDGE THE RIVER STOPPED FLOWING ... A GREAT DISTANCE AWAY! IN THE MIDDLE OF THE RIVER THE PRIESTS STOOD ON DRY GROUND.

3. This miracle is reminiscent of what other miracle, and why is this important at this point? See Exodus 14:21–22; 15:8; Joshua 4:23–24.

CROSSING THE RED SEA. THIS EXALTS JOSHUA IN THE EYES OF THE ISRAELITES AS IT DID MOSES CROSSING THE RED SEA.

DAY FOUR—COMPLETING THE STORY, AND NEVER FORGETTING IT (JOSH. 4)

1. Joshua 4 has two main parts, the first found in the chapter's mid-section.

   a. Note each phrase in Joshua 4:10–18 that fulfills the promise in Joshua 3:7.

   THE PRIESTS REMAINED STANDING
   IN MIDDLE OF JORDAN UNTILL
   EVERYTHING WAS DONE

   THE PEOPLE HURRIED OVER

   THE PRIESTS CAME TO THE OTHER
   SIDE.

   THE ARMY CROSSED OVER.

   THE PRIESTS CAME OUT OF
   THE RIVER + THE WATER
   RETURNED.

   b. Why was it important at this point to confirm Joshua as the one through whom God was leading his people as he had in the past?

   BECAUSE THEY WERE ABOUT
   TO DO SOME REALLY HARD
   STUFF! CONFIDENCE IN
   THEIR LEADER REQUIRED
   THEM TO IT WAS GOD
   LEADING THEM + PROTECTING
   THEM.

2. Joshua 3:12 began a part of the story not completed until Joshua 4:1–9, 19–24. The most literal translation of verse 9 is, "And Joshua set up twelve stones in the midst of the Jordan, in the place where the feet of the priests bearing the ark of the covenant had stood." So verses 8–9 would indicate two piles of stones: one in the middle of the river, and one at Gilgal, their new encampment (Josh. 4:19–20). What was the purpose of these stones, according to 4:6–7 and 4:21–23?

TO SERVE AS A MEMORIAL FOR THEIR DESCENDENTS TO KNOW GOD DRIED UP THE JORDAN AS HE DID THE RED SEA.

3a. What do you notice about the two central purposes of God stated in the final verse (Josh. 4:24)?

1) THE HAND OF LORD IS POWERFUL
2) ALWAYS FEAR THE LORD YOUR GOD.

b. Compare Joshua 4:24 with Exodus 14:29–31. What do you learn about God's good purposes here?

THE VERY SAME:
GOD'S POWER
FEAR THE LORD

DAY FIVE—WE MUST NOT FORGET

1. A remnant of God's people has never stopped being faithful in remembering and passing on the wonders of God—even to us. Read 2 Timothy 1:1–14. What wonders have occurred, and in what ways do Paul and Timothy show us how to remember and pass on those wonders?

FAITH PASSED ON BY ANCESTORS,
GOD'S SPIRIT IS ONE OF POWER,
LOVE + SELF-DISCIPLINE.
CALLED TO A HOLY LIFE FOR
HIS PURPOSE + BY HIS GRACE.
DEATH DESTROYED BY CHRIST

2. In all his wonderful works, God's purposes continue to be that the peoples of the earth might know his mighty hand and that his people might fear him forever (Josh. 4:24). Again in 2 Timothy 1:1–14, how do these same purposes motivate Paul? How might they even more strongly motivate you?

   HE IS ABLE TO SUFFER FOR THE SAKE OF THE GOSPEL. BECAUSE HE KNOWS GOD PAUL BELIEVES GOD.

3. Let us conclude with the encouragement of God's presence and leading as we seek to receive, guard, and pass on all the wonders of his salvation. Reread Joshua 3:3–4 and prayerfully thank God for the loving encouragement these verses give.

Notes for Lesson 3

Lesson 4 (Josh. 5-6)

GOD LEADS TO
VICTORY—HIS WAY!

The Israelites have finally crossed over into the promised land. But they cannot just move in and settle down; they have to take possession of it (Josh. 1:11). And they must do it God's way. Mercifully, God makes every step of that way clear. What is required of them is to listen and to obey. May we understand the same requirement for us!

DAY ONE—SEE THE WHOLE STORY

Read through Joshua 5–6, which present all the important ingredients of the first crucial victory west of the Jordan. How might you organize this Scripture into titled sections?

Pick one verse from each of your sections to write down and think about further.

JOSHUA 5

V.1 FEAR OF ISRAELITES + THEIR GOD WHO DRIED UP JORDAN RIVER.

• CIRCUMCISION OF POST EGYPT ISRAELITE MEN

VS 7 "SO HE RAISED UP THEIR SONS IN THEIR PLACE + THESE WERE THE ONES JOSHUA CIRCUMCISED."

• PASSOVER, END OF MANNA + BEGINNING OF EATING FOOD OF THE LAND

VS 12 "THE MANNA STOPPED THE DAY AFTER THEY ATE THIS FOOD FROM THE LAND."

• JOSHUA ENCOUNTERS COMMANDER OF THE ARMY OF THE LORD

VS 15 "THE COMMANDER OF THE LORD'S ARMY REPLIED, 'TAKE OFF YOUR SANDALS FOR THE PLACE WHERE YOU ARE STANDING IS HOLY'"

JOSHUA 6 • THE LORD DELIVERS JERICHO INTO JOSHUA'S HANDS

VS 2 ...

• JOSHUA COMMANDS FULFILLMENT OF OATH TO RAHAB

VS 22 ...

40

Day Two—First, Remember the Covenant God (Josh. 5:1–12)

No enemies met the Israelites on the Jordan's west bank, as Joshua 5:1 explains. Rahab was right (see Josh. 2:8–11). However, instead of rushing into military confrontation, the Israelites pause to observe two ceremonies commanded by God. Read through Joshua 5:1–12.

1. First, circumcision. What can we learn about the significance of circumcision in Genesis 17:1–14?

   IT IS A SIGN OF GOD'S COVENANT WITH ABRAHAM.
   A FLESH SIGN OF AN EVERLASTING COVENANT.
   TO NOT BE CIRCUMCISED IS DISOBEDIENCE TO GOD + COVENANT.

2. Why might it seem practically foolish to undergo this rite at this point?

   A 40 YR BACKLOG! ☺
   A LOGISTICAL NIGHTMARE!

3. Why is the background in Joshua 5:2–8 important in our understanding of the God in charge of this story?

> HE DOESN'T CHANGE.
> HE HONORS THE COVENANT.
> HE EXPECTS HIS PEOPLE TO
>   HONOR THE COVENANT AS WELL.

4. Second, the Passover. Now that the "reproach of Egypt" is "rolled away" (i.e., they are no longer slaves in a foreign land, but rather a nation of God's people in their own land), they pause for one more ceremony. According to Exodus 12:1–14, 24–28, 47–49, what was the purpose of the yearly Passover celebration?

> A REMINDER OF WHEN THE LORD
> PASSED OVER THE ISRAELITE HOMES,
> WHILE THEY WERE CAPTIVE IN
> EGYPT, SPARED THE KILLING OF
> ALL THEIR 1ST BORN MALE
> CHILDREN. ALL OF EGYPT'S 1ST BORN
> SONS WERE KILLED AS GOD
> STRUCK DOWN THE CAPTORS OF
> HIS PEOPLE.

5. The fourteenth day of the first month is the day designated by Moses to celebrate the Passover. Read Joshua 5:10–12 and comment on the amazing timing and provision of God for his people.

THE 14TH WAS THE EVENING OF PASSOVER; NOT ONLY SET FREE FROM THEIR CAPTORS BUT EATING FROM THE LONG PROMISED LAND.

6. These two ceremonies God commanded as signs to remind his people that they belong to a God who has chosen them, redeemed them, and covenanted faithfully with them. Why are these reminders crucial at this point?

THIS WAS THE FULFILLMENT OF A PROMISE TO ABRAHAM, THEN TO MOSES. ISRAELITES WERE ENTERING THE PROMISED LAND + NEEDED TO REMEMBER THIS WAS OF GOD.

Day Three—It's His Battle
(Josh. 5:13–6:14)

1a. Joshua receives his battle instructions in person. What words or details tell you about this one who appears to Joshua (Josh. 5:13–15)?

JOSHUA LOOKED UP. MAN APPEARED WITH A DRAWN SWORD. HE WAS NOT FOR JOSHUA OR HIS ENEMIES. HE WAS THE COMMANDER OF THE LORD'S ARMY (+FOR THE LORD).

HOLY GROUND

HID HIS FACE

b. What strikes you about this scene in comparison with Exodus 3:1–6?

TAKE OFF SANDALS – STANDING ON HOLY GROUND!

HID HIS FACE

44

2. Joshua 6 continues this scene, with a brief interjection
   (v. 1) regarding Jericho's being tightly shut against God's
   people. Then, in Joshua 6:2–5, this commander tells
   Joshua the plan. What surprising elements do you find
   in these marching orders? JERICHO
   ALREADY DELIVERED INTO JOSHUA'S
   HANDS. MORE OF REPETITIVE
   PARADE THAN A MILITARY
   STRATEGY.

3. Comment on the role of the ark of the covenant in the
   narrative and in the military strategy (Josh. 6:6–14).

   THE WORD, SPIRIT OF GOD
   CIRCLED THE CITY.

4. Clearly, these seven days of marching are days of sacred procession, perhaps even part of the Feast of Unleavened Bread, which continued for the seven days following the Passover meal, as a sign of Israel's consecration to the Lord (see Ex. 12:15–20). What might be the effects of such marching on the Israelites themselves? On the people in Jericho?

> ISRAELITES: THE POWER OF GOD'S PRESENCE. OBEYING GOD EVEN WHEN IT MADE NO SENSE. AN EXAMPLE OF FAITH & OBEDIENCE.

5. It was indeed the Lord's battle, the Lord's strategy, the Lord's victory. But what was required of the people? See Hebrews 11:30.

> BY FAITH THE WALLS OF JERICHO FELL!

DAY FOUR—A CLIMAX WITH TWO SIDES (JOSH. 6:15–27)

1. The seventh day, the seventh time around the city, with the seven priests blasting on their seven trumpets . . .

46

a great shout rises, the walls collapse, and the Israelites charge in. But Joshua's order is clear concerning what is "devoted" to the Lord, or "under the ban"—that is, given over entirely to God, often through total destruction. What do the following verses tell us of this practice?

a. Joshua 6:17–21, 24

THE ENTIRE CITY OF JERICHO WAS 'DEVOTED' TO THE LORD, EXCEPT FOR RAHAB AND HER FAMILY WITH HER IN HER HOUSE AND ALL SILVER, GOLD, BRONZE + IRON ARE SACRED TO THE LORD.

b. Deuteronomy 20:16–18

DO NOT LEAVE ALIVE ANY LIVING THING.

2. Such utter destruction is difficult to take in. How should we regard these people who lost their city and their lives? According to Genesis 15:12–16, what was God's perspective, as he told Abraham long before about this coming back to the land to defeat the Amorites? *Note: "Amorites" and "Canaanites" are often used as general names for the land's inhabitants.*

THEIR SIN APPARENTLY HAD REACHED ITS FULL MEASURE.

3. Such destruction by fire gives a vivid picture of the way God ultimately will judge those who reject him and his ways. But another vivid picture parallels the one of judgment. Find every mention of Rahab in Joshua 6:17–25. Why do you think these verses are arranged this way? What do these verses teach us about God's mercy?

GOD SPARES THOSE WHO RESPOND TO HIM WITH FAITH EVIDENT IN DEED. AS RAHAB PROFESSED WHO GOD IS AND SERVED TO PROTECT HIS SERVANTS, GOD SPARED HER LIFE + THAT OF HER HOUSEHOLD WITH HER!

4. Rahab and her family were brought "outside the camp" (Josh. 6:23) because they were ceremonially unclean according to Mosaic law. But they found a permanent home among God's people.

   a. Whom did Rahab marry, according to Matthew 1:4–5?

   SALMON

   b. What do we know about her husband's family from Matthew 1 and Numbers 7:2, 12?

   DESCENDENT OF ABRAHAM, TRIBE OF JUDAH
   LEADERS IN THEIR TRIBE

   c. Whom does Scripture identify as Rahab's son, and whom did he marry (Matt. 1:5; cf. Ruth 4:13–22)?

   BOAZ – SON OF SALMON + RAHAB – WHO MARRIED RUTH – DAUGHTER-IN-LAW OF NAOMI + A MOABITE

d. Who, as we saw previously, was the promised end of this family line (Matt. 1:16)?

Jesus!

5. Rahab's blessing stands alongside the cursing of Jericho in the text. Read and comment on Joshua 6:26 along with 1 Kings 16:34.

YIKES. OATH FULFILLED WHEN HIEL (OF BETHEL) REBUILT JERICHO UNDER WICKED KING AHAB.

DAY FIVE—TAKING OFF OUR SANDALS

1. Look back and see where we've come in this lesson on a battle ordained, enacted, and concluded according to God's divine plan. List, with brief explanations, the attributes of God that have emerged through this story.

GOD FULFILLS HIS PROMISES.

GOD IS PRESENT.

GOD GOES BEFORE

GOD IS HOLY

GOD RESPONDS TO FAITH/BELIEF IN WHO HE IS WITH SPARING FROM DESTRUCTION.

2. This God has appeared to us as he appeared to Joshua— only fully, in the flesh, to bear God's judgment for our sin and to mercifully offer us eternal life. Who is this holy Lord, before whom we should fall to the ground in reverence? How do the following verses reveal the Lord Jesus Christ as the fulfillment of the covenant of circumcision and as the fulfillment of the Passover celebration carried

out by the Israelites? Who do the completed Scriptures reveal him to be?

a. Matthew 26:17–19, 26–29

APPOINTED IN TIME; THE TEACHER; OBSERVER OF PASSOVER.

HIS BODY-THE BREAD OF PASSOVER.
HIS BLOOD-THE WINE OF PASSOVER
POURED OUT FOR MANY FOR THE
FORGIVENESS OF SINS. HE IS THE
BLOOD OF THE COVENANT.

b. Colossians 2:9–15

JESUS IS THE FULLNESS OF THE DEITY
IN BODILY FORM.
HE IS THE CIRCUMCISION OF MY
SINFUL NATURE.
CHRIST MADE ME ALIVE, FORGAVE ALL
MY SIN, PAID ALL MY DEBT
HE DISARMED ALL POWERS AND
AUTHORITIES + NAILED THEM
TO A CROSS.

c. Revelation 19:11–16

RIDES THE WHITE HORSE
CALLED FAITHFUL + TRUE
JUDGES + MAKES WAR (WITH JUSTICE)
EYES BLAZING FIRE
WEARS MANY CROWNS
UNKNOWN NAME WRITTEN ON HIM
WEARING ROBE DIPPED IN BLOOD
NAME IS THE WORD OF GOD.
KING OF KINGS + LORD OF LORDS

Notes for Lesson 4

Lesson 5 (Josh. 7–8)

GOD TAKES SIN SERIOUSLY

From Jericho to Ai . . . from victory to defeat . . . from the story of one family spared to that of one family destroyed . . . these chapters give us a sobering reminder that God's people cannot blithely move on to victory without dealing with the sin in their hearts and in their midst. May we, as we study, be sobered by the reminder of how seriously God takes sin.

DAY ONE—A DISGRACEFUL THING IN ISRAEL (JOSH. 7:1–15)

1. The move from Jericho to Ai was a strategic one, up from a central fortress of the Jordan Valley to a smaller but centrally located fortress of the hill country. But the focus of the narrative is not on military strategy. Read the first verse and the last verse of Joshua 7: what is the crucial context for this story?

THE LORD'S ANGER BECAUSE ACHAN TOOK SOME OF THE DEVOTED THINGS. HE WAS UNFAITHFUL.

2. What similarities and differences do you note between the description of the conquest of Jericho and the description of the conquest in Joshua 7:2–5?

S - SPIES SENT FIRST. THEY CAME BACK WITH REPORT

D - CONFIDENCE IN THEMSELVES RATHER THAN IN GOD. 36 KILLED THEN REMAINDER WERE DEFEATED. THE PEOPLE MELTED WITH FEAR AND 'BECAME LIKE WATER.'

3. What similarities and differences do you note between Joshua's cry to God in Joshua 7:6–9 and the various cries in Numbers 14:1–19?

S - MOSES + JOSHUA BOTH TORE THEIR CLOTHES AND FELL ON THEIR FACES BEFORE THE ARK OF THE COVENANT IN PRAYER TO GOD. WOULD RATHER HAVE STAYED THAN BE WHERE THEY ARE.

D - MOSES STILL HAD CONFIDENCE IN GOD JOSHUA DID NOT.

4. What truths about human sin can we learn from God's response to Joshua in 7:10–15?

GOD DOES NOT TOLERATE A LITTLE BIT OF SIN + DISOBEDIENCE. EVEN A LITTLE BRINGS ABOUT DESTRUCTION/DEFEAT BY THE ENEMY

5. What similarities might you note between this story and that of Ananias and Sapphira in Acts 5:1–11?

> DISOBEDIENCE, DISCEPTION, TRUTH REVEALED/CONFESSED, PUNISHMENT BY GOD.

DAY TWO—GOD JUDGES SIN (JOSH. 7:16–26)

1. First, read Joshua 7:16–26.

2. When Achan is singled out according to God's pre-scribed method, he obeys Joshua's command to "give glory to the LORD God" by admitting what he has done. What strikes you in his confession (Josh. 7:20–21)?

> "SINNED AGAINST THE LORD, GOD OF ISRAEL..."
>
> SAW THE PRETTY THINGS
>
> COVETED THEM
>
> TOOK THEM
>
> HID THEM

3. According to Joshua 7:12–13, 15, how did Achan's punishment justly answer his sin?

WHATEVER IS DEVOTED TO DESTRUCTION MUST BE DESTROYED.

WHOEVER IS CAUGHT WITH DEVOTED THINGS MUST ALSO BE DESTROYED.

4a. How did God oppositely but similarly deal with Rahab and Achan (see Josh. 7:24)?

BECAUSE RAHAB BELIEVED + OBEYED SHE WAS NOT DEVOTED TO DESTRUCTION. RATHER, SHE WAS TAKEN IN, PROTECTED AND BLESSED BY GOD + HIS PEOPLE. GOD'S PEOPLE HAD TO DESTROY ACHAN. NOT SO WITH RAHAB.

b. In what ways do faith and disobedience bring far-reaching consequences to family and community?

BLESSING FOR FAITH RIPPLE THROUGH COMMUNITIES + GENERATIONS.

PUNISHMENT FOR DISOBEDIENCE DOES LIKEWISE!

5. The scene in Joshua 7:24–26 is dreadful and difficult to take in. But here Israel raises up another pile of stones as

they had done before. Of what would this pile of rocks remind them and their children (and us)?

DISOBEDIENCE BRINGS ABOUT
DESTRUCTION.

DAY THREE—GETTING IT RIGHT THIS TIME (JOSH. 8:1–29)

1. How do the first two verses of Joshua 8 strike you, in the wake of Joshua 7?

CONFUSING A BIT. JOSHUA
MUST HAVE BEEN AFRAID +
DISCOURAGED, UNDERSTANDABLY, OR GOD WOULD
NOT HAVE SAID "DO NOT BE AFRAID;
DO NOT BE DISCOURAGED"... THEY
JUST HAD TO STONE + BURN A
FAMILY WHO DISOBEYED, A FAMILY
OF THEIR OWN PEOPLE. THAT'S
MUCH HARDER THAN THE PLUNDER
OF ENEMIES.

2. Read Joshua 8:3–23, and contrast the God-ordered but very different methods of taking Jericho and taking Ai. What do you make of this contrast?

NO SPIES - 30K STRAIGHT TO BATTLE. GOD INSTRUCTED STRATEGIC AMBUSH, LURING MEN OF AI OUT OF THE CITY. PERHAPS OBEYING GOD IN EVERY BATTLE IS THE MESSAGE + EACH ONE IS UNIQUE.

3. What parts of the narrative affirm that the attack of Ai is God-directed?

GOD KNEW KING OF AI WOULD LEAD HIS ARMY OUT OF CITY. GOD GAVE ISRAEL THE CITY OF AI. GOD TOLD JOSHUA TO HOLD OUT HIS JAVELIN TOWARD AI + GOD WOULD GIVE THE CITY INTO THE HANDS OF JOSHUA.

4. In regard to "devoting" the conquered city to the Lord, how do God's instructions concerning Ai differ from those concerning Jericho (Josh. 8:2, 24–27)? *Note: The text does not explain, but several scholars have suggested that all the riches of Jericho were to be an offering of the "firstfruits" of the land to the Lord; see Deuteronomy 26:1–4.*

THIS TIME ISRAEL WAS INSTRUC- TED TO TAKE FOR THEMSELVES THE LIVESTOCK + PLUNDER OF AI.

5. The events of Joshua 8:28–29 are meant to be a sign of God's judgment on nations that had turned against him. How might Deuteronomy 9:4–6 give context for these verses and for the whole story of Ai?

GOD DRIVES OUT + DESTROYS NATIONS OF WICKEDNESS. IT IS NOT DUE TO ISRAEL'S RIGHTEOUSNESS OR INTEGRITY FOR THEY REMAIN A STIFF-NECKED PEOPLE.

DAY FOUR—RENEWING THE COVENANT
(JOSH. 8:30–35)

1. For background, read Deuteronomy 11:26–32 and Deuteronomy 27:1–28:14. Then read Joshua 8:30–35. What do we know about God from reading these two passages?

BLESSING FOR OBEDIENCE
CURSE FOR DISOBEDIENCE

GOD TAKES OBEDIENCE
VERY SERIOUSLY!

2. From Ai the Israelites had marched northward on a road along the ridge of the mountains until they reached two distinct mountain peaks, on either side of the city of Shechem (see map #2). What would the people have known about this spot, according to Genesis 12:6–7?

ABRAHAM, WHO PITCHED HIS TENT
BETWEEN AI + BETHEL, WAS TOLD
BY GOD HE + HIS DESCENDENTS
WOULD BE GIVEN THIS LAND,
A LAND FLOWING WITH MILK AND
HONEY.

3. Mt. Ebal and Mt. Gerizim together create an amazing natural amphitheater, so that, as the tribes gathered on the slopes of these mountains, apparently everyone could hear. If God can part the Red Sea and the Jordan, he can do this! Picture the scene: a huge outdoor worship service. List the order of worship as you see it in Joshua 8:30–35.

BUILT AN ALTAR (ACCORDING TO GOD'S
                            INSTRUCTIONS)
OFFERINGS
COPIED LAW ONTO THE STONES
ALL THE PEOPLE STOOD WATCHING
   1/2 TOWARD ONE MT; 1/2 TOWARD THE
      OTHER MT
JOSHUA READ THE LAW

4. Of what were the people being reminded through the altar of sacrifice and the reading of the blessings and the curses?

OF GOD'S AUTHORITY + S.OVEREIGNTY

5. What parts of this scene evidence God's rich mercy and grace?

DAY FIVE—STANDING TOGETHER
BEFORE GOD'S WORD

1. How does Hebrews 10:19–31 apply many of the lessons of Joshua 7–8 to us as New Testament Christians?

   PERSEVERE IN FAITH

   TO KEEP SINNING WHEN TRUTH
   IS KNOWN IS EVEN WORSE
   THAN THE PUNISHMENT FOR
   THOSE WHO REJECTED THE
   LAW OF MOSES. IT IS A
   DREADFUL THING TO FALL
   INTO THE HANDS OF THE
   LIVING GOD.

2a. Achan hid his sin, and the truth had to be forced out of him. According to 1 John 1:8–9, what should we do with our sin?

   WE ARE TO CONFESS OUR SIN.
   HE IS FAITHFUL TO FORGIVE US
   OF OUR SIN + CLEANSE US FROM
   ALL UNRIGHTEOUSNESS.

b. How can God be just, as 1 John 1:9 says, and still forgive us? See 1 John 2:1–2.

JESUS CHRIST IS OUR ADVOCATE
& ATONING SACRIFICE BEFORE
THE FATHER.

3. What sins are most easy for us to hide and bury the evidence? Whom does such pretense affect?

OURSELVES — OUR RELATIONSHIP
WITH THE FATHER — AND THOSE
AROUND US.

PRIDE
ENVY
GREED
LUST

4. Let us finish by opening our hearts in prayer to God, who is rich in mercy and who has made a way, through Christ, for our complete forgiveness.

Notes for Lesson 5

Lesson 6 (Josh. 9–10)

GOD MEANS FOR
US TO ASK

God means for us to "ask counsel from" or to "inquire of" him, as Joshua 9:14 puts it. Joshua 9 offers an example of what happens when we do not, and Joshua 10 offers an example of what happens when we do. Not because anything depends on us, but because everything depends on God, our proper role is to go to him and humbly ask him for wisdom and help. May this lesson encourage us to do so, more and more.

DAY ONE—READING THE STORY (JOSH. 9)

Joshua has returned to Gilgal as a secure base camp. Meanwhile (Josh. 9:1–2), all the cities in the hills and mountains are joining forces against him and against God. But one group, led by the Gibeonites, tries a different tactic. Read the story in Joshua 9, jotting down observations and comments.

A RUSE-
GIBEONITES WENT AS DELEGATION.
APPEAR POOR; DISGUISE; PRETEND
TO BE FROM DISTANT COUNTRY;
CLAIM TO BE "YOUR SERVANTS."
LIE-

ISRAELITES DID NOT INQUIRE OF
THE LORD. THEY MADE A TREATY W/THEM
INSTEAD, AN OATH BEFORE GOD. THEN
ISRAELITES WERE BOUND TO NOT DESTROY
THEIR NEIGHBORS IN THE PROMISED LAND
+ INSTEAD MADE THEM SERVANTS.

DAY TWO—LEARNING FROM THE STORY (JOSH. 9)

1. How are Deuteronomy 7:1–2 and Deuteronomy 20:10–
   18 helpful in understanding Joshua 9?

   ISRELITES WERE TOLD THAT
   THE LORD INSTRUCTED THEM
   TO TOTALLY DESTROY THE
   INHABITANTS OF THE LAND AND
   MAKE NO TREATY WITH THEM.
   OTHERWISE, THE 7 TRIBES
   WILL TEACH ISRAELITES
   DESTESTABLE THINGS.

2. If the Gibeonites and the Israelites were standing before
   you, and you were asked to give an evaluation of their
   respective actions throughout this story, what would you
   say to each? As you write your two short addresses, refer
   to specific verses from the text.

3. The "house of the Lord" refers to the moveable tabernacle God had instructed his people to build in the wilderness. The tabernacle represented God's presence with his people, with the ark of the covenant at its center. At the tabernacle, priests offered regular sacrifices to God on behalf of the people, for which much wood and water was required. How did the Gibeonites' sentence include great mercy? See Joshua 9:21, 26–27 and Psalm 84:10.

THEY SERVED THE "HOUSE OF THE LORD". THEY WERE NOT SLAVES TO ISRAELITES PERSONALLY. NOR WERE THEY SLAUGHTERED.

4. The tabernacle resided successively through the years at Shechem, Shiloh, Gibeon, and finally as the temple in Jerusalem. Hundreds of years later, when God's people returned from exile to rebuild their fallen temple, what can we notice in Nehemiah's report (Neh. 3:7; 7:25)?

REFERRED TO AS MEN OF ~~THE~~ ISRAEL. THEY HELPED REBUILD THE TEMPLE.

Day Three—Not on Our Own
This Time (Josh. 10:1–15)

The Israelites made a treaty without inquiring of God, but they still have to honor it. They also face the consequences of it. As they do so, however, in Joshua 10, their leader this time is listening to—and speaking to—God.

1. Read Joshua 10:1–5, and look again at maps 2, 3, and 4. Why have these kings of the southern territory become so alarmed?

   GIBEON WAS AN IMPORTANT LARGE CITY W/ GOOD FIGHTERS. + NOW THEY WERE W/ ISRAEL.

2. God emerges as the central character in this story. From Joshua 10:6–15, write down everything you can observe and learn about God.

- GOD GAVE THE AMORITES INTO THE HANDS OF THE ISRAELITES.
- GOD SAID "DO NOT BE AFRAID OF THEM."
- THE LORD THREW THE AMORITES INTO CONFUSION
- THE LORD PUMMELED + KILLED THEM WITH LARGE HAILSTONES.
- THE SUN STOOD STILL + MOON STOPPED - THE LORD LISTENED TO A HUMAN BEING (JOSHUA). THE LORD FOUGHT FOR ISRAEL.

71

3. Also from Joshua 10:6–15, how does Joshua faithfully play his part in God's plan?

> HE WAS NOT AFRAID

4. However it worked, the miracle is that God divinely intervened in the movement of the planets. The miracle also is that our God mercifully listens to our prayers. What do the following verses tell us about prayer?

   a. Psalm 66:16–20

   > HE LISTENS + HEARS OUR PRAYERS

   b. Proverbs 15:8, 29

   > PRAYER PLEASES GOD (OF THE UPRIGHT) GOD HEARS THE PRAYERS OF THE RIGHTEOUS.

c. Hebrews 10:19–22

BECAUSE OF CHRIST, WE CAN
HAVE CONFIDENCE TO ENTER THE
MOST HOLY PLACE - TO DRAW
NEAR TO GOD

d. James 5:13–16

PRAY IN ALL CIRCUMSTANCES!
CONFESS SIN TO EACH OTHER
SO WE MAY BE HEALED. FOR
THE PRAYERS OF A RIGHTEOUS
PERSON IS POWERFUL & EFFECTIVE.

DAY FOUR—SUBDUING THE SOUTH
(JOSH. 10:16–43)

The rest of Joshua 10 completes this battle and—at lightning speed—all the rest of the battles in the southern campaign.

1. Read Joshua 10:16–28. What Joshua did with these five kings who had marched against God's people was meant to be symbolic for "all the men of Israel" (v. 24). What were they meant to learn at this symbolic moment?

2. It is important to apply such scenes rightly! God's people in our day do not make up a nation meant to subdue other nations and lands. But we are a people, and we have an enemy against which to fight. According to the following verses, who is that enemy, and how do we fight?

    a.   Ephesians 6:10–18

    b.   1 Peter 5:8–9

3. How are our battles similar to those of the Israelites in Joshua's day?

4a. Read Joshua 10:29–39, listing the cities conquered, one by one, in this campaign.

b. How does this chapter's conclusion (vv. 40–42) clearly reiterate God's role and Joshua's role?

5a. Read the following verses, and write down their recurring theme: Exodus 14:13–14; Deuteronomy 1:26–31; 3:21–22; Joshua 10:14; 10:42.

b.   What are the implications of these verses for you?

DAY FIVE—ASKING COUNSEL FROM GOD

It would seem appropriate to pray, on the final day of this study. Look back through days 1 through 4; perhaps you will want to write several brief prayers based on verses you have studied this week. Perhaps you need to spend time asking God for wisdom and help. What a privilege to inquire of him, according to his Word. Let us thank God for the miracle of prayer—that our God hears and responds to the prayers of his people.

Notes for Lesson 6

Lesson 7 (Josh. 11:1–13:7)

GOD HAS DONE IT!

It is good to see we are at the end of the war! Joshua 11–12 finishes it and then looks back to recount God's faithful accomplishment of what he promised. With all the looking forward that occupies our minds, we will do well to look back, with God's people, and see the faithful hand of God.

DAY ONE—ONE MORE BATTLE (JOSH. 11:1–15)

1. The northern kings now assemble, and they make an imposing enemy. What is the effect of all the various details included in Joshua 11:1–5?

2. According to Joshua 11:6–8, how is the victory explained?

3a. According to the following verses, why might God have instructed his people to burn the chariots and hamstring the horses (i.e., cut their leg tendons, preventing them from walking)?

Psalm 20:7

Isaiah 31:1

b. Have you known a situation where the normal props are taken away, providing an opportunity to seek help from the Lord? If you have, briefly describe that situation.

4. First, read once more Deuteronomy 20:16–18. With this as context, what do you see as the main thrust of Joshua 11:10–15, as it is told to us? Refer to specific phrases from the text.

5. As he leads his people into the land, obedience to God's law stands out as the mark of greatness in Joshua. How does Joshua connect to the "Joshua to come" in this regard? See John 8:28–29.

DAY TWO—SUMMING UP THE CONQUEST
(JOSH. 11:16–23)

1. Read Joshua 11:16–23. In what ways does this section constitute a beautiful conclusion to the first eleven chapters of the book? A quick look back to Joshua 1 will be helpful.

2. Joshua 11:18 briefly summarizes several years (approximately five to seven) of hard work. How does this verse give an important reminder within the flow of the book, and how does this verse give an important reminder to us as God's people now? See Exodus 23:27–30 and Hebrews 10:35–36.

3. Along with his mercy (which we have seen to God's people, to Rahab and her family, and to the Gibeonites), God's judgment on those who reject him is clear in this story. Read Romans 1:18–32. How do these verses help explain the words of Joshua 11:20? Recall also Genesis 15:16.

4a. The whole land was claimed by God's people because they had conquered all the specific and strategic places listed in Joshua 11:16–17. Parts of the land remained to be subdued, as mentioned in Joshua 11:22 and as we shall see in Joshua 13. But, at this point, Joshua takes time to highlight those Anakites who had been destroyed. From the following verses, what do we know of the Anakites?

Numbers 13:31–33

Deuteronomy 1:26–28; 9:1–3

Joshua 11:21–22

b. What clear lesson lies here for us, as we, too, face over-whelming challenges and battles?

DAY THREE—ALL THESE KINGS (JOSH. 12)

1. Quickly read through Joshua 12. What are your first impressions?

2. Why do you think Scripture takes time for detailed lists such as these?

3. Joshua 12:7–24 summarizes the conquests we've read about in Joshua. Why do you think the account begins with verses 1–6, which rehearse battles from Numbers 21:21–35?

4. Think back over the last year of your life. Take time to say and/or write a prayer of thanksgiving, recounting God's works, less in the form of "thank you for blessing me" and more in the detailed manner of Joshua 12.

Day Four—From Taking to Possessing

1a. According to Joshua 11:23 and Joshua 12:7, what did Joshua do with the land God gave the people?

b. Read the background commands in Numbers 26:52–56.

2. Why is the land referred to consistently as an "inheritance" of the tribes of Israel, in the law and in Joshua? (Joshua 11:23 is one of more than forty times the word "inheritance" appears in this book.) To answer, look back to Genesis 12:7 one more time.

3. Read Joshua 13:1–7. This chapter introduces a long section of the book describing Joshua's distribution of the inheritance. He was called by God not only to take the land but also to allocate it to the tribes, and that task is not yet done—although he is probably by now eighty-five to one hundred years old. Joshua 13:2 begins a listing of specific parts of the land not yet conquered (mostly along the Mediterranean coast and in the far north). And yet Joshua 13:6b–7 reiterates the command to distribute all the land to his people. The whole land has been given to them, but many of the tribes will have to fight and conquer parts of what they receive.

As the people of God now, how do we experience this tension between the war that has been won and the battles that still have to be fought?

4. Read Psalm 136, and relish the celebration of the inheritance in its larger context. How does the focus of this whole psalm lift our eyes and our perspective?

Day Five—Celebrating Our Inheritance

1. How does the New Testament explain our inheritance as the people of God, now that the promised Joshua has already come?

   a. John 3:16

   b. John 14:1–6

    c.   2 Corinthians 1:21–22

    d.   1 Peter 1:3–5

    e.   Revelation 21:1–7

2. If you can do so from your heart, write your own statement concerning your inheritance in Christ.

Notes for Lesson 7

Lesson 8 (Josh. 13:8–19:51)

GOD GAVE IT; HIS PEOPLE MUST CLAIM IT!

According to his word, God has given his people the land. Now, God tells them to subdue and settle in it—also according to his word. Will they do it? Would we? Will we, having been given all things in Christ, persevere faithfully until the end?

DAY ONE—GOD WORKS THROUGH TRIBES AND LOTS (JOSH. 13:8–14:5)

We have already seen God's command to distribute and subdue the land (Josh. 13:1–7; day 4 of lesson 7). Joshua 13–19 offers a detailed account of which tribes got what and how they dealt with what they got. The rest of Joshua 13 deals just with the tribes east of the Jordan; Joshua is consistently careful to include them with the people of God.

1. Look through Joshua 13:8–33 to find

    a. which two-and-a-half tribes had been given land east of the Jordan.

    b. the first mention of failure to destroy the enemies in their assigned territory.

2. Let's stop and remember who these tribes are. For background, find in each of the following passages the names of the twelve sons of Jacob, who was named Israel, as well as the total number of Israelites. This question will explain the title of the fourth book of the Bible.

    a. Genesis 46:1–27 (leaving Canaan for Egypt, in Joseph's day)

b. Numbers 1:17–46 (in the wilderness, the second year after Moses led them out of Egypt)

c. Numbers 26 (just before entering the promised land)

3. To clarify: how do we get a total of twelve tribal territories if the tribe of Levi gets no land? See Genesis 48:3–6 and Joshua 14:1–5.

4. The Levites, who worked in the temple and received no land inheritance, got to learn what truth that each of us should learn? See Joshua 13:33, Deuteronomy 18:1–2, and Psalm 73:25–26.

5. Having summarized in Joshua 13:8–33 the allotment of the land east of the Jordan, Joshua moves into an explanation of the land west of the Jordan—Canaan, the promised land. The eastward land had earlier been assigned by Moses, as God directed him. As Joshua 14:1–5 tells us, the westward land was now assigned by lot, as God had commanded. What good results might this God-ordained method have?

a.   Psalm 16:5

b.   Proverbs 19:21

DAY TWO—CALEB AND HIS TRIBE . . . FOLLOWING
GOD'S PLAN (JOSH. 14:6–15; 15:13–19)

1. The allotment of land west of the Jordan begins with a
   special portion for Caleb. Review the role of Caleb in
   Numbers 13:1–14:9.

2. Now read Caleb's sequel in Joshua 14:6–15 and Joshua
   15:13–19. Write a list of the phrases that stand out; how
   does each help to define Caleb's character?

3a. How do you think the example of Caleb challenged the Israelites?

b. How, specifically, does his example challenge you?

4. Caleb is part of the tribe of Judah, which is given its inheritance first, even though Judah was not the oldest son of Jacob.

a. How do Jacob's final blessings of his sons in Genesis 49:1–12 help to explain this?

b. Revelation 5:5–14 also tells of the "Lion of the tribe of Judah." How do these verses show the fulfillment of that prophecy in Genesis 49:9–10?

5. The previous question should remind us that all the detailed Old Testament records of genealogy were for a significant purpose. How would you summarize the importance for these Israelites of following the seed of Abraham?

DAY THREE—SOME NOT FOLLOWING
GOD'S PLAN . . .

1. We have seen one mention of the Israelites not driving out the people in this land, as they had been told to do (Josh. 13:13). What do you note in the following progression of verses?

   a. Joshua 15:63

   b. Joshua 16:10

   c. Joshua 17:12–13

2. What brief and positive example is inserted in Joshua 17:3–6? See the background in Numbers 27:1–11. What are your comments?

3. The tribes of Joseph's two sons not only did not drive out the Canaanites; they also complained about their lot, apparently wanting more already-cleared, conquered, and ready-to-be-inhabited space. What do you think of Joshua's response in Joshua 17:14–18?

4. What should these people have remembered? See Deuteronomy 7:17–26 and Exodus 23:27–33.

5. What can we remember, as we face huge challenges in our obedience to God's Word?

a. 2 Corinthians 1:8–9, 21–22

b. Philippians 2:12–13

c. 2 Peter 1:3–4

DAY FOUR—JOSHUA SHOWS HOW TO OBEY (JOSH. 18)

1. In Deuteronomy 12:4–14, what important instructions had Moses given concerning worship in the new land? God's "Name" implies the ark of the covenant, the symbol of his presence with his people. The ark dwelt in the tabernacle, or "Tent of meeting."

2. Many of the tribes faltered not just in conquering the cities of their territories but even in claiming their territories to begin with. What significant course of action does Joshua take in Joshua 18:1–10?

3. Shiloh remained the center of Israelite worship for many years (see I Sam. 1:1–3). Look back through the last few pages. Why was one central place of worship so important?

4. Read Joshua 18:11 through Joshua 19 to see the completion of the allotment of the land. What beautiful completion is found in Joshua 19:49–51?

DAY FIVE—THE RESPONSE GOD DESIRES

Psalm 105 reviews the story of the Israelites who finally received the land promised them.

1. On this final day, read through and relish this psalm.

2. Write down several themes you find in Psalm 105 that connect to the story in Joshua.

3. Why did God give his people the land, according to this psalm?

4. What responses to such a God are called for in Psalm 105?

Notes for Lesson 8

Lesson 9 (Josh. 20-22)

GOD SETTLES HIS PEOPLE— ACCORDING TO HIS WORD

Whenever a nation newly establishes itself, the people have to work out how they will get along. This nation has already been given its complete law through Moses; now, as they settle in, they have to apply that law with obedience and care. What a lesson for us as God's people who have been given the complete Scriptures; may we take the utmost care to live together obediently according to his Word.

DAY ONE—THE LORD PROVIDES A REFUGE (JOSH. 20)

1. First, read the background passages in Numbers 35:9–34 and Deuteronomy 19:1–13. Then read of the Israelites' obedience in Joshua 20.

2. What does God's emphasis on these cities of refuge tell us about his divine character and nature?

3a. When, and only when, could an offender leave a city of refuge, free from fear of harm?

b. Read Hebrews 9:11–14 and Hebrews 10:11–14. What has our great High Priest done for us?

DAY TWO—THE LORD PROVIDES
FOR HIS WORKERS (JOSH. 21)

1. First, read the background in Numbers 3:1–13 and Numbers 35:1–8.

2. In Joshua 21:1–3, how do the Levites follow the good example of Caleb and the daughters of Zelophehad? What can we learn from these examples?

3. Levi had three sons: Kohath, Gershon, and Merari. The line of Kohath developed two branches: one the descendants of Aaron, who were the priestly line, and "the rest of Kohath's descendants" (Josh. 21:5). Read through Joshua 21:1–42, and notice how carefully organized it is, according to these three Levitical lines. If you like, check out the total number of Levitical towns with God's command in Numbers 35:7.

4. According to Moses' final words concerning the Levites in Deuteronomy 33:9b–10, why might God have scattered them in cities throughout the land?

5. How does this Old Testament provision for the Levites transfer to a New Testament provision for those who serve the church? See 1 Corinthians 9:1–14.

DAY THREE—NOT ONE . . . (JOSH. 21:43–45)

1. Joshua 21: 43–45 concludes the allotment section, just as Joshua 11:16–23 concluded the conquest section. What a beautifully written book! What great themes

of the book are strongly reaffirmed here? Again, you might want to look back to Joshua 1.

2a. What words in these verses affirm the completion and fullness of what has been accomplished?

b. What do these words tell us about God?

3. Many commentators have noted how this picture of victory over enemies points ahead to the final, complete victory to come. As we look back to this historical picture and ahead to the final reality, how should we respond? See 2 Thessalonians 1:6–10.

DAY FOUR—THE FINAL SETTLING (JOSH. 22)

Joshua 22 is a wonderful story of God's people seeking to follow his word and learning to do it together. Read through this chapter carefully, relishing the story's details. Then, for Joshua, for the two and a half eastern tribes, and for the remaining Israelites, write your observations concerning their efforts to serve God with all their heart and soul, according to his word. Refer to particular verses.

DAY FIVE—THE CHALLENGING PICTURE
OF GOD'S PEOPLE TOGETHER

1a. What an encouraging picture of the people of God sharing and settling the land. For each of this week's chapters (Josh. 20–22), consider and briefly explain how the central role of worship (through tabernacle, ark, altar, priest, etc.) is crucial to what the chapter is about.

b. From the beginning of the book, how has this been true? How has God consistently led his people to keep the worship of him at the center of their lives?

2a. In light of these chapters, summarize how God's people are meant to live in relation to God and to each other.

b. How does Hebrews 10:19–25 offer a New Testament perspective on this question?

Notes for Lesson 9

Lesson 10 (Josh. 23–24)

GOD'S PEOPLE ARE
CALLED TO RESPOND

Two great gatherings of God's people bring to a close Joshua's life, this book, and this crucial period of conquest. Through Joshua, God has led them to take the land; now they must get ready to possess and settle all of it in obedience and faithfulness to the Lord. Joshua's two farewell addresses challenge us to respond as well.

DAY ONE—THE FIRST FINAL FAREWELL SPEECH
(JOSH. 23)

1. First, picture the scene as described in Joshua 23:1–2. Then, having read through the entire chapter, respond to the following questions, referring to specific verses in your answers.

2. What does Joshua's speech say about the past?

3. What various commands does Joshua give the people to follow? Is any one central?

4. Depending on whether or not the people follow Joshua's commands, what two very different sets of consequences will follow?

Day Two—One More Impassioned Speech
(Josh. 24:1–13)

Joshua's second farewell speech is similar to the first, although it is more detailed and demands a definite response from the people.

1. How does Joshua 24:1–2 show the more formal and solemn nature of this gathering?

2. God's review of their history is amazing! Read Joshua 24:2–13, divide the text into four titled sections, and then write down several careful observations from each section. Background references are provided in case you wish to consult them.

   a. Section title: _____

   Verses: _____

   See Genesis 12:1–9

b.   Section title: _____

   Verses: _____

   See Exodus 1–14

c.   Section title: _____

   Verses: _____

   See Numbers 21:21–24:25

d.   Section title: _____

   Verses: _____

   See Joshua 1–11

3. Through reviewing this history in Joshua 24:2–13, what is God showing about himself?

4. What phrases from the following verses stand out (Josh. 23:14; 21:45; Num. 23:16–20)?

DAY THREE—NOW, THE CHARGE
(JOSH. 24:14–15)

1a. Consider Joshua's charge in verses 14–15. What does he do in the first sentence?

b. What does he do in the last sentence?

c. What are the choices involved, in the middle?

2. We have already read of Abraham's time at Shechem (Gen. 12:1–9). According to Genesis 35:2–4, what did Jacob do at Shechem, the place of this gathering in Joshua 24?

3. In Romans 12:1–2 and Ephesians 2:1–10, how might Paul's words be considered a kind of New Testament version of the speech in Joshua 24:2–15?

DAY FOUR—THE PEOPLE ANSWER
(JOSH. 24:16–27)

1a. Is the response in Joshua 24:16–18 a good one? How so?

b. How can you explain Joshua's response in Joshua 24:19–20?

c. He continues to challenge them. What is Joshua after, in verses 21–24? Does he get it?

2. How do we see this same sobering caution in the New Testament?

a. Luke 14:25–33

b. John 21:15–19

3. Joshua asks the people to make a covenant commitment before God (Josh. 24:25–27).

   a. What other similar ceremonies have we seen in this book?

   b. What is the primary focus in this ceremony (Josh. 24:25–27) and in every similar ceremony?

   c. Is it not amazing that God had his servants write all these things down so that the words can speak to us as well? Meditate on the following verses:

      • Romans 15:4
      • 2 Timothy 3:14–17
      • Revelation 22:6–7, 18–19

4. In the final verses of Joshua, what do you find that beautifully concludes the theme of the land being given by God to his people as their promised inheritance?

5. How does Joshua 24:29, 31 perfectly conclude Joshua's climactic command to serve the Lord in Joshua 24:14–15?

DAY FIVE—WHAT IS THE END OF THIS STORY?

1. God has been faithful to his promises. The challenge has
    been given for God's people to be faithful. According to
    the following verses, how much resolution do we find at
    the end of this book?

    a. Joshua 24:31

    b. Look through Judges 1 and 2, focusing on Judges
        2:1–5, 10–15.

2. Clearly, Joshua has not given us the final, happy end
    to the whole story, but rather a foretaste of that end.
    We have seen all along how this promised land points
    ahead to our rich inheritance in Christ Jesus, wholly
    received by faith but still to be completed when Jesus
    comes again to reign and dwell forever with all his

people in a new heaven and earth. That is God's good promise to us, when we receive by faith the great gift of salvation in our Lord and Savior Jesus Christ. In light of all God's good promises, now, how shall we live?

a.   Joshua 1:7–9

b.   Joshua 22:5

c.   Joshua 23:6–8, 11

d. Joshua 24:14

Notes for Lesson 10

NOTES FOR LEADERS

What a privilege it is to lead a group in studying the Word of God! Following are six principles offered to help guide you as you lead.

1. THE PRIMACY OF THE BIBLICAL TEXT

If you forget all the other principles, I encourage you to hold on to this one! The Bible is God speaking to us, through his inspired Word—living and active and sharper than a two-edged sword. As leaders, we aim to point people as effectively as possible into this Word. We can trust the Bible to do all that God intends in the lives of those studying with us.

This means that the job of a leader is to direct the conversation of a group constantly back into the text. If you "get stuck," usually the best thing to say is: "Let's go back to the text and read it again. . . ." The questions in this study aim to lead people into the text, rather than into a swirl of personal opinions about the topics of the text; therefore, depending on the questions should help. Personal opinions and experiences will often enrich your group's interactions; however, many Bible studies these days have moved almost exclusively into the realm of "What does this mean to me?" rather than first trying to get straight on "What does this mean?"

We'll never understand the text perfectly, but we can stand on one of the great principles of the Reformation: the *perspicuity* of Scripture. This simply means *understandability*. God made us word-creatures, in his image, and he gave us a Word that he wants us to understand more and more, with careful reading and study, and shared counsel and prayer.

The primacy of the text implies less of a dependence on commentaries and answer guides than often has been the case. I do not offer answers to the questions, because the answers are in the biblical text, and we desperately need to learn how to dig in and find them. When individuals articulate what they find for themselves (leaders included!), they have learned more, with each of their answers, about studying God's Word. These competencies are then transferable and applicable in every other study of the Bible. Without a set of answers, a leader will not be an "answer person," but rather a fellow searcher of the Scriptures.

Helps *are* helpful in the right place! It is good to keep at hand a Bible dictionary of some kind. The lessons themselves actually offer context and help with the questions as they are asked. A few commentaries are listed in the "Notes on Translations and Study Helps," and these can give further guidance after one has spent good time with the text itself. I place great importance as well on the help of leaders and teachers in one's church, which leads us into the second principle.

2. THE CONTEXT OF THE CHURCH

As Christians, we have a new identity: we are part of the body of Christ. According to the New Testament, that body is clearly meant to live and work in local bodies, local churches. The ideal context for Bible study is within a church body—one that is reaching out in all directions to the people around it. (Bible studies can be the best places for evangelism!) I realize that these studies will be used in all kinds of ways and places; but whatever the context, I would hope that the group leaders have a layer of solid church leaders around them, people to whom they can go with questions and concerns as they study the Scriptures. When a leader doesn't know the answer to a question that arises, it's really OK to say, "I don't know. But I'll be happy to try to find out." Then that leader can go to pastors and teachers, as well as to commentaries, to learn more.

The church context has many ramifications for Bible study. For example, when a visitor attends a study and comes to know the Lord, the visitor—and his or her family—can be plugged into the context of the church. For another example, what happens in a Bible study often can be integrated with other courses of study within the church, and even with the preaching, so that the whole body learns and grows together. This depends, of course, on the connection of those leading the study with those leading the church—a connection that I have found to be most fruitful and encouraging.

3. The Importance of Planning and Thinking Ahead

How many of us have experienced the rush to get to Bible study on time . . . or have jumped in without thinking through what will happen during the precious minutes of group interaction . . . or have felt out of control as we've made our way through a quarter of the questions and used up three-quarters of the time!

It is crucial, after having worked through the lesson yourself, to think it through from the perspective of leading the discussion. How will you open the session, giving perhaps a nutshell statement of the main theme and the central goals for the day? (Each lesson offers a brief introduction that will help with the opening.) Which questions do you not want to miss discussing, and which ones could you quickly summarize or even skip? How much time would you like to allot for the different sections of the study?

If you're leading a group by yourself, you will need to prepare extra carefully—and that can be done! If you're part of a larger study, perhaps with multiple small groups, it's helpful for the various group leaders to meet together and to help each other with the planning. Often, a group of leaders meets early on the morning of a study, in order to help the others with the fruit of their study, plan the group time, and pray—which leads into the fourth principle.

4. THE CRUCIAL ROLE OF PRAYER

If these words we're studying are truly the inspired Word of God, then how much we need to ask for his Spirit's help and guidance as we study his revelation! This is a prayer found often in Scripture itself, and a prayer God evidently loves to answer: that he would give us understanding of his truth, according to his Word. I encourage you as a leader to pray before and as you work through the lesson, to encourage those in your group to do the same, to model this kind of prayer as you lead the group time, to pray for your group members by name throughout the week, and to ask one or two "prayer warriors" in your life to pray for you as you lead.

5. THE SENSITIVE ART OF LEADING

Whole manuals, of course, have been written on this subject! Actually, the four principles preceding this one may be most fundamental in cultivating your group leadership ability. Again, I encourage you to consider yourself not as a person with all the right answers, but rather as one who studies along with the people in your group—and who then facilitates the group members' discussion of all they have discovered in the Scriptures.

There is always a tension between pouring out the wisdom of all your own preparation and knowledge, on the one hand, and encouraging those in your group to relish and share all they have learned, on the other. I advise leaders to lean more heavily toward the latter, reserving the former to steer gently and wisely through a well-planned group discussion. What we're trying to accomplish is not to cement our own roles as leaders, but to participate in God's work of raising up mature Christians who know how to study and understand the Word—and who will themselves become equipped to lead.

With specific issues in group leading—such as encouraging everybody to talk, or handling one who talks too much—I encourage you to seek the counsel of one with experience in leading groups. There is no better help than the mentoring and prayerful support of a wise person who has been there! That's even better than the best "how-to" manual. If you have a number of group leaders, perhaps you will invite an experienced group leader to come and conduct a practical session on how to lead.

Remember: the default move is, "Back to the text!"

6. THE POWER OF THE SCRIPTURES TO DELIGHT

Finally, in the midst of it all, let us not forget to delight together in the Scriptures! We should be serious but not joyless! In fact, we as leaders should model for our groups a growing and satisfying delight in the Word of God—as we notice its beauty, stop to linger over a lovely word or phrase, enjoy the poetry, appreciate the shape of a passage from beginning to end, laugh at a touch of irony or an image that hits home, wonder over a truth that pierces the soul.

May we share and spread the response of Jeremiah, who said:

> Your words were found, and I ate them,
> and your words became to me a joy
> and the delight of my heart. (Jer. 15:16)

OUTLINE OF JOSHUA

I. Preparation This Side of the Jordan (Josh. 1-2)
   A. Joshua Gives the Word (Josh. 1)
   B. Rahab and the Spies (Josh. 2)

II. Crossing the Jordan (Josh. 3-4)

III. Conquering the Land on the Other Side (Josh. 5-12)
   A. Preparation of the Covenant Ceremonies (Josh. 5:1-12)
   B. The Lord's Battle at Jericho (Josh. 5:13 – 6:27)
   C. Curses and Blessings of Disobedience and Obedience (Josh. 7-8)
      1. Acted out in Ai (Josh. 7:1 – 8:29)
      2. Read on the Mountains (Josh 8:30-35)
   D. Learning to Seek God for the Battle (Josh. 9-11)
      1. The Gibeonites (Josh. 9)
      2. Following the Lord through the South (Josh. 10)
      3. And the North (Josh. 11)
   E. All These Defeated Kings (Josh. 12)

IV. Receiving the Inheritance of the Land (Josh. 13-19)
   A. Joshua Gives God's Plan (Josh. 13:1-7)
   B. Inheritance East of the Jordan (Josh. 13:8-33)
   C. Inheritance West of the Jordan (Josh. 14-19)

Suggested
Memory Passages

Only be strong and very courageous, being careful to do according to all the law that Moses my servant commanded you. Do not turn from it to the right hand or to the left, that you may have good success wherever you go. This Book of the Law shall not depart from your mouth, but you shall meditate on it day and night, so that you may be careful to do according to all that is written in it. For then you will make your way prosperous, and then you will have good success. Have I not commanded you? Be strong and courageous. Do not be frightened, and do not be dismayed, for the Lord your God is with you wherever you go.

Josh. 1:7–9

Thus the Lord gave to Israel all the land that he swore to give to their fathers. And they took possession of it, and they settled there. And the Lord gave them rest on every side just as he had sworn to their fathers. Not one of all their enemies had withstood them, for the Lord had given all their enemies into their hands. Not one word of all the good promises that the Lord had made to the house of Israel had failed; all came to pass.

Josh. 21:43–45

Notes on Translations and Study Helps

This study can be done with any reliable translation of the Bible, although I recommend the English Standard Version for its essentially literal but beautifully readable translation of the original languages. In preparing this study, I have used and quoted from the English Standard Version, published by Crossway Bibles in Wheaton, Illinois.

These lessons are designed to be completed with only the Bible open in front of you. The point is to grapple with the text, not with what others have said about the text. The goal is to know, increasingly, the joy and reward of digging into the Scriptures, God's breathed-out words, which are not only able to make us wise for salvation through faith in Christ Jesus but also profitable for teaching, reproof, correction, and training in righteousness, that each of us may be competent, equipped for every good work (2 Tim. 3:15–17). To help you dig in, basic and helpful contexts and comments are given throughout the lessons. I have used and learned from the following books in my study and preparation; you may find sources such as these helpful at some point.

General Handbooks

The Crossway Comprehensive Concordance of the Holy Bible: English Standard Version. Compiled by William D. Mounce. Wheaton, IL: Crossway, 2002. Other concordances are available from various publishers and for different translations.

The Illustrated Bible Dictionary. 4 vols. Wheaton, IL: Tyndale House Publishers, 1980. *The Zondervan Pictorial Encyclopedia of the Bible* is similarly helpful.

Ryken, Leland, James Wilhoit, and Tremper Longman III, eds. *Dictionary of Biblical Imagery.* Downers Grove, IL: InterVarsity Press, 1998.

Ryken, Leland, Philip Ryken, and James Wilhoit. *Ryken's Bible Handbook.* Wheaton, IL: Tyndale House Publishers, 2005.

Vine's Complete Expository Dictionary of Old and New Testament Words. Nashville: Thomas Nelson, 1984.

Commentaries

Calvin, John. *Calvin's Commentaries.* Vol. 4, *The Book of Joshua.* Grand Rapids: Baker, 1984.

Davis, Dale Ralph. *Joshua: No Falling Words.* Ross-shire, Great Britain: Christian Focus, 2000.

Hess, Richard S. *Joshua: An Introduction and Commentary.* Tyndale Old Testament Commentary Series. Downers Grove, IL: InterVarsity, 1996.

Madvig, Donald H. *Joshua.* The Expositor's Bible Commentary Series. Grand Rapids: Zondervan, 1992.

Woudstra, Marten H. *The Book of Joshua.* The New International Commentary on the Old Testament Series. Grand Rapids: Eerdmans, 1981.

Kathleen Nielson (MA, PhD in literature, Vanderbilt University) has taught in the English departments at Vanderbilt University, Bethel College (Minnesota), and Wheaton College. She is the author of numerous Bible studies, the book *Bible Study: Following the Ways of the Word*, and various articles and poems. Kathleen has directed and taught women's Bible studies at several churches and speaks extensively at conferences and retreats. She serves as advisor and editor for The Gospel Coalition and was its director of women's initiatives from 2010–2017. She is also on the board of directors of The Charles Simeon Trust.

Kathleen and her husband Niel have three sons, two beautiful daughters-in-law, and a growing number of grandchildren!

Learn How to Understand and Apply the Old Testament

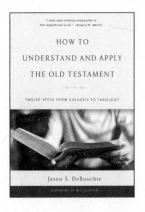

For anyone looking to interpret the Old Testament wisely and well, Jason DeRouchie provides an extensively field-tested and logical twelve-stage process to deepen understanding and shape theology (biblical, systematic, and practical), taking us from an analysis of a passage's genre all the way to its practical application. Loaded with examples and practical answers, the twelve chapters will empower believers to study, practice, and teach the Old Testament as *Christian* Scripture, understanding and applying it in ways that nurture hope in the gospel and magnify the Messiah.

"Conversationally engaging; literarily transparent; materially comprehensive; pedagogically superb; academically sound, precise, and informed—all this and more. In over fifty-two years of teaching in the classrooms of higher education, I have seen nothing comparable to this magnificent work by DeRouchie—destined to be the classic in its field."
—**Eugene H. Merrill**, Distinguished Professor Emeritus of Old Testament Studies, Dallas Theological Seminary